Guy, Angel and the Missing Egg

Book 2 of the Guy and Angel Travel in Time Series

Chris Crawley

Tudman Press

Copyright © 2023 Chris Crawley

All rights reserved

The characters and events portrayed in this book are fictitious. Any similarity to real persons, living or dead, is coincidental and not intended by the author.

No part of this book may be reproduced, or stored in a retrieval system, or transmitted in any form or by any means, electronic, mechanical, photocopying, recording, or otherwise, without express written permission of the publisher.

ISBN: 9798865114536
Imprint: Independently published

Cover design by: Mallette Blum
Library of Congress Control Number: 2018675309
Printed in the United States of America

For my mum, Marion Claudette, who gave me my love of history and introduced me to the suffragettes.

Contents

Title Page
Copyright
Dedication
Introduction
Coming Soon...
Theft of an Egg   1
Chapter 1 – Saturday 22nd October   3
Chapter 2 – Sunday 23rd October   7
Chapter 3 – Thursday 23rd October 1913   10
Chapter 4 – Friday 24th October 1913   16
Chapter 5 – Saturday 25th October 1913   42
Chapter 6 – Sunday 26th October 1913   53
Chapter 7 – Monday 27th October 1913   64
Chapter 8 – Tuesday 28th October 1913   75
Chapter 9 – Wednesday 29th October 1913   80
Chapter 10 – Thursday 30th October 1913   95

Chapter 11 – Friday 31st October 1913	111
Chapter 12 – Saturday 1st November 1913	118
Chapter 13 – Sunday 2nd November 1913	136
Chapter 14 – Monday 3rd November 1913	145
Chapter 15 – Tuesday 4th November 1913	167
Chapter 16 – Wednesday 5th November 1913	208
Chapter 17 – Sunday 23rd October	228
Chapter 18 - Monday 24th October	232
Epilogue	235
Histotical Context	241
Guy and Angel Travel in Time	243
About the Author	245

Introduction

Chris Crawley weaves together real historical events and people with fictitious characters. It should be stated that whilst many of the people in this book did actually exist, the conversations are imagined and were created for the purpose of this story.

This is Book 2 of the Guy and Angel Travel in Time Series.

A Faberge egg was stolen from a family in the past, so Angel transports Guy back to 1913 and together they try to track down and retrieve the missing jewel and bring it back to the present.

Let the journey continue...

Coming Soon...

Guy, Angel and the Elusive Painting

Theft of an Egg

"Claude, take Beattie and hide, quickly," whispered Beatrice. "There's a good boy, don't cry, don't be scared, it will be fine, I know what they want. They won't hurt us."

There was another loud thump on the door of the little flat in Coronation Buildings, South Lambeth, London.

"Mummy, are they going take you away?" Claude was shaking as he grabbed his little sister's hand.

"No darling, I have something very valuable, and they want it. Now quickly, hide under the bed and don't come out until I say so. Go, now!" Beatrice pushed Claude and Beattie in the direction of the bedroom.

Several loud thumps landed on the door as five-year-old Claude, dragged a bewildered two-year-old Beattie, into the bedroom and under the double bed. Claude hugged his little sister tight. Beattie began to cry as they heard voices shouting and furniture being dragged around. Claude tried to soothe her into being quiet, but he was crying himself. The front door slammed, the little flat shook and footsteps came running into the bedroom.

"Claude, Beattie come out darlings, it's fine they have gone." Beatrice ran to the bed and helped them out, scooping them up in her arms. "Mummy's fine, the nasty men just wanted my pretty blue egg, they took it, but we are all safe and that's what matters."

The little group cuddled up on the bed, Beatrice singing them a lullaby, as much to soothe herself as her children.

Chapter 1 – Saturday 22nd October

"And that Mrs Devereux, is how Ottomar, my grandfather, found them when he got home from work later that night, all three of them, cuddled up on the bed asleep," said Barbara as she took a sip of her tea. "Claude, my father, remembered the terror of that afternoon all his life. It happened on the 31st October 1913, he used to tell us the story every Hallowe'en."

Barbara reached across the table to take another cake from the stand. "Ottomar was German, and a waiter at the Gordon's Hotel on Trafalgar Square. It was popular back then to be a German waiter in London, I don't know why. Of course, the next year he was deported, you know when World War One broke out. Quite sad really as he was made to fight for Germany, and he didn't make it back. Killed on the Somme in 1916. I never got to meet him."

"Oh, my goodness, that is such a sad story,"

said Katrina Devereux. "I'm sure Beatrice was sadder about losing her husband than her Faberge egg, but she literally had her nest egg stolen from her. She might have made some money from selling it, you know, when she was widowed."

"Well absolutely. That egg was probably worth quite a bit and she was entitled to it. It had been gifted to her when she left service in 1907 to get married." Barbara signalled to the waitress across the little tea shop. "Can you bring another pot of English Breakfast please dear. Thank you.

"Beatrice looked after a very wealthy old lady in Westminster, her name was Elizabeth Towers. She thought the world of Beatrice and not having any children of her own, she wanted to look after her."

"What is a Faberge egg?" asked Guy, slightly confused.

"They are little enamel eggs, covered in gold and jewels, made by a Russian jeweller called Carl Faberge, he made them for the Tsar of Russia to give to his wife."

"Oh, cool, thanks, never heard of them to be honest," said Guy, putting a little chocolate cake on his plate. "Did Beatrice suspect who had taken it?"

"Well, yes, as a matter of a fact she did. Elizabeth's nephew was angry about the Faberge egg going to Beatrice, he thought he was going to get it in her will. Of course, when she died it wasn't there. He heard a rumour from the staff that it had been given to Beatrice, so he reported her to the police as having stolen it." Barbara shook her head before taking a deep breath and continuing.

"The police investigated and found that she had a solicitor's letter and a letter of ownership, it proved the egg had been gifted to her and she was now the legal owner. The old lady had thought of everything, except she didn't realise the lengths her nephew would go to in order to get it back. It was quite likely that the men who broke into her flat were hired to steal it."

The little trio paused their conversation to think about poor Beatrice and the stolen egg, munching on their cakes as they did so.

"Some people are so wicked," said Katrina shaking her head. "And now your little great granddaughter needs an operation, just imagine if the Faberge egg was still in the family, it could be worth a small fortune. You could have sent her off to the USA, no problem."

"Well, I suspect it would have been worth a small fortune, it was brought back from Russia in the 1890s by Elizabeth's husband. It had been gifted to him by the Tsar himself. He was a silk trader if I remember rightly, not sure how he met the Tsar though," Barbara stopped to drink some tea. "Yes, it surely would have been enough to send Chloe off to the USA." She wiped her eyes, "I just don't know what we are going to do to be honest."

"Have you thought of crowd funding?" asked Guy,

"No, what is that? Do you think it would work?" asked Barbara.

"It might," said Guy, "it's worth a go. I'm happy to meet up with your family and explain it."

"Thank you, Guy, if you would, anything that helps."

"No problem, we can meet up tomorrow, after church. It's my half term holiday so I have got a bit of time this week."

"We'd all really appreciate that," said Barbara taking Guy's hand and squeezing it.

Chapter 2 – Sunday 23rd October

"You are a good lad Guy," said Gramps, folding the newspaper so that he could start his crossword. "Let's hope this crowd funding thing works."

"Oh, I do hope so," said Grandma. "They are a lovely family and Chloe is such a sweet child."

"I think it'll work," said Mark confidently, looking up from his laptop and pausing his game.

"We can but try," said Guy, setting his watch to five kilometres. "I'm just off out for a run, won't be long. I'm looking forward to that roast dinner I can smell cooking."

"Don't be late," called Grandma after him as he went out the front door. "You don't want to eat it cold."

Guy wondered which way to run, dusk was settling in, it was raining a little and he didn't fancy getting muddy, so he headed round the Lakeview Estate to the main road into the little town of Chalk Hill. When he reached the town, he headed straight to the cemetery and his dad's grave. He found it a comfort to have a few words with his dad every week, bring his dad up to speed on what had been going on. His dad was also the only one he could tell his inner most thoughts about Angel to, as Guy's escapade in the seventeenth century was a complete secret from everyone else.

"It's ridiculous Dad, but I miss her so much," Guy sighed and looked at a magpie that had landed nearby, he was relieved when a second magpie landed too. "One for sorrow, two for joy, as Gramps always says." Guy smiled, and then turned his attention back to his dad.

"I only knew Angel for short a space of time, I spent hardly any time with her really and yet I will never forget her. I don't think any other girl will ever match up to her. She was so thoughtful and kind to everyone, she was also brave, she really took a chance taking me back in time," The church bell chimed six times, Guy looked at his running watch and took it off pause. "Well Dad, Grandma is cooking a roast, so I had better head back, you know what she's like."

Resuming his run into the smaller churchyard, he said hello to Michael Cooper's grave. Guy was still convinced this was the grave of the boy he had been kidnapped with in the seventeenth century.

"One of these days Michael, I am going to research your life and find out for sure. I'd love to know how you made it back."

Running back to the Lakeview Estate, past the woods by the actual chalk hill, listening to music and planning his latest BTEC Sports Science assignment in his head, Guy wasn't really paying attention to the weather. If had been, he would have seen the trees around him bending and swaying in the wind. As he ran, he suddenly realised his feet were not on the floor, he was running in mid-air, he began to spin round as his breath was taken away by the wind. He knew exactly what was happening, as he floated down to the ground he looked around for Angel. He landed with thump on the grass, the road and the buildings having disappeared and there before him was the girl he had thought constantly about for the last month. Angel Jasmine.

Chapter 3 – Thursday 23rd October 1913

"It's 1913, isn't it?" said Guy.

"It is," confirmed Angel.

"We are going after the Faberge egg, aren't we?"

"You know me so well," laughed Angel.

"Please tell me there is some underwear in that bag this time, and not just a loincloth." Guy pointed to Angel's brown leather holdall.

Angel put the holdall down, moved a button on the gold-coloured clasp, opened the bag with a chuckle to herself, and began to rummage around inside.

"Oh, there is underwear alright," said Angel with a wide grin. She pulled out a pair of what looked like woolly leggings and a matching white t-shirt style top. "Long Johns, they'll keep you warm."

"Wonderful, after last time I'm not

complaining," said Guy looking around for somewhere suitable to change. "What else have I got?"

"White shirt, dark grey suit, black waistcoat, black shoes, black tie and a peaked cap."

"Thanks, nice, different. You look very smart." Guy took in Angel's navy-blue ankle-length skirt and long line jacket, which she wore with a crisp white blouse underneath. The whole outfit was topped by a blue hat with a small brim and navy-blue gloves.

"Thank you," said Angel, adjusting the hat over her afro, which had been pulled back into a low chignon.

"What day is it?" asked Guy.

"It's Thursday 23rd October," replied Angel.

"Oh, so you still can't perform time travel in anything but years?" Guy smiled, as Angel handed his clothes to him.

"Well, actually I can," said Angel, her head held high. "I have been training, but to be honest, I thought we would need the time to locate Ottomar and Beatrice and find out where they live. The Faberge egg is stolen on 31st October, that gives us plenty of time to get everything planned and ready to steal the egg back."

"I guess you're right, but I'm supposed to be

back at school on Hallowe'en. In fact, I'm going to a Hallowe'en fancy dress party on Saturday the 29th."

"Ok, well on your return I will deliver you back to just after the moment I took you," said Angel, looking confident in her newfound skill.

"That would be amazing, because my grandma has a roast on and I really didn't want to miss it," said Guy laughing as he walked over towards some hedges. "Won't be a moment, I'll change over here."

Guy emerged from the hedge looking very dapper in his suit and ready to face life in 1913.

"It would be great if we didn't get separated this time," said Guy handing Angel his clothes, watch, phone, earphones and trainers. "I mean there were times when I really didn't think I'd ever see you again, or anyone else for that matter."

"Definitely, let's stick close together this time, no early morning runs round St. James' Park for you." Angel shut her bag and gathered the handle ready to go.

"Trust me, I have no intention of going for an early morning run," Guy shuddered remembering his encounter with the kidnappers. "No, let's just get the egg and get out!"

"I think we should make our way into London now, we can stay in a hotel tonight, but then I was thinking that we should get jobs at Ottomar's hotel tomorrow," said Angel. "What do you say Guy? Are you up for a bit of pot washing? I could be a chambermaid."

"Good idea, I just wish that I could add all this work experience to my CV." They both laughed. "The hotel is on Trafalgar Square, it must be a big one, so it might have staff rooms for us to sleep in."

"Yeah, that would be useful," replied Angel. "Which way to the nearest train station?"

"Well Chalk Hill definitely had a station in Victorian times, so that should be the nearest, it runs through Brentwood and on to London, Liverpool Street. I think it will be the same now in 1913. Only one way to find out."

*

Guy and Angel walked the short distance into Chalk Hill, the village green and church were familiar to Guy, although the Catholic church, Guy's church, was not yet built.

"One moment Angel, I just want to check something," Guy headed into the churchyard and Michael Cooper's grave, which was there, as it always was. "Hi Michael, Beth, I knew you would be here, I just wanted to say hello from 1913, no idea why."

"You think that is Michael, the boy you were

kidnapped with? But he lived in Upminster."

"I know, but he married someone called Beth and it looks like they had a son called Guy, too much coincidence."

"I see what you mean," said Angel looking at the gravestones.

Making their way back into Chalk Hill, Guy saw the centre looked no different, the shops around the green had different names, but they were still the same buildings. However, the houses around the centre had not yet been built, meaning Chalk Hill was still a village rather than a town in 1913. The train station was exactly the same from outside, apart from the Chalk Hill sign, which instead of being black writing on a white background with a red and white railway logo, was white writing on a black background.

The entrance hall was how Guy remembered it from when he was little, before it had been decorated, with the little ticket office that had a wooden window. They purchased their tickets from a man in a smart black uniform, just in time to get on a train to London.

The large black Great Eastern Railway steam engine was puffing away ready go. Guy opened the wooden door and indicated for Angel to get onboard, he followed, and they found some seats in a third-class compartment. Almost immediately the whistle blew and the train chugged away from the station, London bound, in a cloud of steam.

"What happened to Terence Harvey-Smythe?" asked Angel. "Did you pay him off? Or did he get arrested?"

"Arrested, thank God. Apparently, he had been money laundering for some time, but his trial doesn't come up until next Easter at the earliest."

"Oh, so what's happened then? To your housing estate I mean?"

"It's all on hold until after his trial. If he is guilty and goes to prison, then the money from Devereux Legacy will be spent on another community project. Grandma and Gramps would like it to go to the local hospice."

"Wow, that's really kind of them, what lovely people."

"They really are. Although, if Harvey-Smythe is found innocent, we shall be using the money to pay off everyone's leases."

"I really hope he goes to prison then, horrible man."

"Definitely, we need to be well shot of him and his casinos."

Guy puffed his cheeks and looked out of the window at the dark Essex countryside rushing past.

Chapter 4 – Friday 24th October 1913

Guy was sitting in the dining room of the Great Eastern Hotel next to Liverpool Street station, he was already tucking into breakfast when Angel came in and joined him. It was a vast room, with a very high ceiling and a central dome, from which hung a beautiful crystal chandelier. The room had a relaxed feeling as the hotel residents ate their breakfast and chatted away to each other.

"Good morning, did you sleep well?" asked Guy, a fork laden with bacon at the ready. "It's very grand here, I don't think we should get too used to this."

"Indeed not," replied Angel, sitting down. "Yes, I did sleep well. I tried not to think about the millions of things that could go wrong. We need a plan, but we need to be flexible too, expect the unexpected."

"I really hope there isn't an unexpected. I'm

still recovering from last time. My leg has a huge scar, and I can still see those decapitated heads on London Bridge." Guy shuddered and had a swig of orange juice.

The waiter took Angel's order, and it wasn't long before she too was enjoying a full English breakfast and orange juice.

"First task then is to secure jobs at the Gordon's Hotel," said Guy. "What if they don't need anyone?"

"They will, I'm sure of it," said Angel confidently, finishing her breakfast. "It's really the only way we can hang around the hotel, find and get to know Ottomar, and not raise too much suspicion."

"Agreed. I mean he is the key really isn't he. We need to find him, in order to find Beatrice and then the egg." Guy put his knife and fork on his plate. "How do we get from here to Trafalgar Square? I suppose we could walk."

"I fancy getting on one of those old open top buses, it will be a laugh." Angel wiped her mouth on a thick white cotton serviette.

"Let's check out of the hotel then and find a bus to Trafalgar Square," said Guy, as he stood up and stepped aside for Angel to lead on.

*

The first thing that hit Guy as they left the

Great Eastern Hotel, was the noise of the traffic, it was so different to what he was used to. The sounds of the engines were familiar, but the clip clop of the horses' hooves echoing on the roads gave a very different atmosphere to the London street. The horse and carts clip clopped alongside the huge motor cars and bicycles weaved in among them, Guy stood for a moment taking the scene in, until Angel nudged his arm and pointed to a bus.

The sign at the front indicated the bus was going to the Strand. Running as fast as they could and weaving in between the many men who were on their way to work in a city office, wearing their black suits and bowler hats, Guy and Angel managed to jump onto the wooden steps, with just seconds to spare. Laughing and rather pleased with themselves, they went up the curved outside steps to the open top deck and sat down in the second row from the front, Angel put her bag on her lap and breathed out in relief.

"Do you want me to take that," offered Guy.

"No, it's fine, I'd best keep it with me, but thanks," replied Angel.

The bus conductor, brushing some dust from his navy uniform, was standing at the front of the top deck and waited until they were underway to start collecting the fares.

"Where to?" he asked Guy.

"The Strand," Guy replied, taking in the

smart peaked cap and brown leather money bag. Angel handed the money over, in return the conductor gave her two tickets and then moved further down the bus.

"These buses look like huge double decker tractors from the front," whispered Guy. "They are seriously impressive machines. And I love the fact they are red London buses, awesome."

Guy pointed to the buses going in the opposite direction, each one covered in advertisements for various products.

"*Cadbury's Cocoa, Pears Soap, the Evening News*. All these adverts are quite familiar to me. *Dewars White Label*, don't know what that one is though," said Guy, craning his neck to read the advertisements on a passing bus. "I also love the fact that everyone wears a hat outside. Mind you Angel, most men on this bus seem to have a boater or a bowler. I've got a cap, that probably means I should be walking."

"A hat does give people a sense of style, doesn't it," said Angel looking at Guy's cap and comparing it to the men in bowlers. "Oh, Guy look at that sign at the front of the bus. *Beware pickpockets, male and female*. Crumbs, nothing changes."

"The *no spitting* sign sounds like good advice," laughed Guy. "I wouldn't want someone's spit landing on my head.

"Quite!" said Angel shuddering. "Also, *No standing under railway bridges,* goodness, why would you stand up on the top deck of a bus whilst going under a bridge?"

"It could knock your head off," said Guy wincing. "Some people just don't think do they."

The bus bounced along very slowly towards the Strand, stopping every so often to let people on and off. Tricycles with baskets on the front cut in front of the buses, making Guy hold his breath. The traffic was very much a mix of horse drawn carts and carriages, alongside motor vehicles, all vying for space on the crowded streets. Pedestrians, both men and women walked in between the traffic, everyone seemed to find their space, but it was making Guy nervous, he had to keep looking away.

"Right, so are we ok to give the egg to Beatrice and Ottomar's descendants then?" asked Guy. "It's been playing on my mind."

"Yes, because we can make changes from the present day, so that's fine, they can have the egg, if we find it."

"Hmm," mused Guy. "But aren't we changing the past for whoever stole the egg, I mean, presumably they sold it and got loads of money. So, if we steal it back, that family will miss out on that money and that will change people's fortunes."

"Guy you're getting good at this and that is a very good question." Angel looked impressed with Guy's thinking. "If whoever took the egg had profited from it, then I wouldn't have been able to bring you back in time, but they didn't," said Angel, with a shrug of her shoulders.

"They didn't make any money from it," repeated Guy. "So, what happened to it?"

"That I don't know," said Angel. "I imagine it was put into hiding somewhere and overtime, for whatever reason, got forgotten about."

"The war breaks out in 1914," Guy lowered his voice. "People got killed, maybe the knowledge of the egg died with someone in the trenches in France." Guy and Angel grimaced. "That's an awful thought, even if they did steal the egg."

"Well, it might not have been that; I really don't know. I got clearance to bring you back, and that means it was never sold," said Angel.

"You got clearance? What's that?" Guy turned away from Fleet Street to face Angel.

"Before I take people back in time, checks have to be run and the checks came back clear – no profit was made."

"Hang on, does that mean no one profited from the Devereux Legacy then," asked Guy, astounded.

"That's right, who knows what those thieves

did with the treasure, but certainly, no one made any life changing amounts of money from it. I reckon they reburied it and then died before they could get back to do anything with it."

"Maybe they were recruited for Cromwell's navy," said Guy with a satisfied laugh. "I looked that up when I got home, it was quite commonplace back then, later on in the seventeenth century it became known as *impressment*, and the recruiters were known as the *press gang*."

"Well, if the people they recruited kept jumping ship, then they would need more people wouldn't they," said Angel rubbing Guy's arm, as she remembered his adventures from a few months earlier.

"Don't lose me this time Angel," said Guy, half laughing and half terrified.

The bus entered the Strand and Guy recognised buildings from the present day. An old Tudor style pub, the Aldwych, even theatres.

"Oh my God, Angel look, it's the Lyceum Theatre. We went there last week to see *The Lion King* for Mark's fifteenth birthday."

"*The Lion King*, was it about animals?"

"Sort of, it's about a lion cub who becomes king of the jungle. It's based on the Disney film," explained Guy. "You have no idea about Disney, do you?"

"Not really," said Angel smiling and shrugging her shoulders.

"We need to get off down by Charing Cross station," said Guy. "It's right by Trafalgar Square."

"Sounds good," Angel said in agreement.

The bus trundled down the Strand, past shops and theatres. As they got close to Charing Cross station, Guy and Angel got up ready to walk down the stairs. The bus stopped and they got off, then made their way towards the giant Nelson's Column in front of them, pigeons scattering and resettling, as they walked across Trafalgar Square.

"Right, we are looking for the Gordon's Hotel," said Angel. "What is Ottomar's surname by the way?"

"I don't know," said Guy sighing in frustration. "He has a wife called Beatrice and children called Claude and Beattie, hopefully that will help."

"Maybe there won't be too many waiters called Ottomar," said Angel with a grimace.

"Let's walk round and try all of the roads leading off from Trafalgar Square," said Guy. "Wow, look at that a real live woman selling bird feed, no way! It's just like *Mary Poppins*."

"Mary who?" asked Angel following Guy. "You mentioned her once before."

"I will tell you all about her later," said Guy.

*

Having walked round every road off Trafalgar Square, Guy and Angel drew a blank.

"No Gordon's Hotel anywhere," said Guy scratching his head under his cap.

"What are we missing?" said Angel, scouring the buildings around her. "Perhaps Gordon's is a chain of hotels."

"Oh, good thinking *Batman*," said Guy.

"*Batman*?" questioned Angel.

"Again, long story, another time," said Guy. "Let's go to all of the hotels that have a view of Trafalgar Square and ask them if they are a Gordon's Hotel."

"Ok, where shall we start? Northumberland Avenue? As it is the nearest," said Angel pointing across the road.

They crossed the road, ducking in between a woman cycling and a horse drawn carriage, then walked to a hotel entrance and looked up.

"The Hotel Victoria," said Guy looking at the large entrance with an arch above it. "It's huge, a good as place to start as any."

Guy and Angel walked through a wooden revolving door into a large foyer. They found themselves standing on a highly polished white marble floor. Four brown and beige marble columns rose up to meet the elaborate ceiling, from which hung an enormous chandelier. They walked into the columned foyer and a little reception booth was in the wall on the right-hand side. Joining the queue, Guy and Angel waited patiently in line until it was their turn.

"Excuse me," said Angel. "Could I ask you a question please?"

The man on reception, who had a badge displaying his name as Edward Pullum, nodded, "Go ahead madam."

"Is this hotel a Gordon's Hotel?" asked Angel.

"Indeed, yes, it is madam, London and New York, finest hotels you will stay in. Would you like to make a reservation?"

"Not exactly," said Angel. "My friend and I are looking for work to be honest and we thought, why not work for a Gordon's Hotel, they have such a fantastic reputation."

The man smiled and looked down at a sheet of paper in front of him.

"Yes, we do have some vacancies. If you would be so good as to wait over there," said the man, pointing to two brown leather Chesterfield sofas facing each other, I will find our housekeeping manager to help you.

Guy and Angel thanked the man and took the indicated seats to wait patiently for further instructions. Five minutes later a woman appeared, she was tall, slim and dressed very tidily in a black dress to her ankles, with black lace up boots looking very polished on her feet. Her hair was pulled back into a bun and her glasses hung on a chain around her neck.

"Miss Liddington," she said, holding out a hand to shake Guy and Angel's. "I understand you are looking for work, please follow me to talk about your previous work experience."

Guy and Angel followed the upright Miss Liddington behind the reception desk and into the staff only area, they were ushered into a small office and sat down on the chairs offered to them. Miss Liddington sat behind her desk and found a notepad and pen, which she dipped into some ink.

"What are your names?" asked Miss Liddington.

"I'm Guy Devereux."

"I'm Angel Jasmine."

"That's an unusual name," said Miss Liddington.

"Yes, it is," said Angel, offering no explanation.

Miss Liddington shook her head and moved on to her next question.

"What work experience do you have?"

"I have worked as a farm labourer quite recently," said Guy.

"Bringing in the harvest?" asked Miss Liddington.

"Yes, in Essex, I'm not afraid of hard work and long hours."

"And you Miss Jasmine?" said Miss Liddington.

"I was working as a dairymaid at the same farm," said Angel.

"I see," said Miss Liddington. "We do have some openings that might suit you, with the Christmas season just round the corner, we shall be very busy over the next few weeks. I can offer you Mr Devereux, work as a kitchen hand. And Miss Jasmine, I am in need of chambermaids. You will both be on trial for a week, so that we can see if you are suitable for us here at the Hotel Victoria, we have very high standards, we are a Gordon's Hotel you know."

Guy and Angel nodded politely; Miss Liddington continued.

"There are some employment terms, which I shall explain. You will work six days a week. Your day off will be a rolling day, so your first day off will be Monday, the next week it will be a Tuesday and so on." Miss Liddington paused to check

Guy and Angel understood, they nodded, and she continued.

"You will have a half day off once a week, this will start on a Wednesday and will also be a rolling half day. Miss Jasmine you will work from six o'clock in the morning to six o'clock in the evening. Mr Devereux, you will work from eight o'clock in the morning to eight o'clock in the evening."

"That sounds very agreeable," said Angel. "Could I just ask, do you have any staff accommodation at all? We are new in London and as yet have nowhere to stay."

"Well, we do have a few rooms, they are very basic, you will be charged and I must stress, this would be on a temporary basis, until you find your own rooms. I can recommend some places for you, mostly in the east or south of London."

"That would be very useful," said Guy. "Thank you."

"Do you have any luggage?" asked Miss Liddington.

"Only my bag," smiled Angel, pointing to her holdall.

"Can you start tomorrow?"

"Yes," said Guy and Angel in unison.

After completing some paperwork, Miss Liddington took Guy and Angel in a staff lift, up to the top of the hotel. She led them along a dimly lit corridor, with no windows and showed them to a little room no bigger and not much more elaborate than a prison cell.

"This is your room Miss Jasmine; this is the women's corridor.

"Thank you, this will be perfect," said Angel, looking at the little iron bed with a grey blanket covering it.

"Report to the housekeeping office at six o'clock tomorrow morning Miss Jasmine. Mr Devereux, I will see you at eight o'clock in my office and I will take you to the kitchen myself. Your uniforms will be provided tomorrow."

"Thank you very much," said Guy. "You won't be disappointed in us; we are hard workers."

"Well, like I said you are on trial, but I do hope you are a hard worker young man," Miss Liddington smiled and left Angel to look around her accommodation. "Mr Devereux, please accompany me to the men's corridor."

Guy was shown to his room and looked around at the white walls and the washstand with a jug and basin. Miss Liddington left him looking at the alarm clock, and raised her eyebrows to indicate he would need to set it.

As soon as she had gone Angel popped her head around the door. "They have thought of everything haven't they."

"Haven't they just," said Guy lifting a china chamber pot from under the bed. "I suppose it is better to have a wee there, than wander around up here in the middle of the night."

"I guess there are no toilets near then, I wonder where we empty it?" said Angel pulling a face. "All will be revealed tomorrow I suppose."

"Let's hope we don't need it. What shall we do this afternoon?" asked Guy, replacing the chamber pot under the bed.

"Well stage one has been done, secure jobs in Ottomar's hotel. I think we should try to find out what we can about the Towers family," said Angel thoughtfully. "It might be useful to be armed with some information."

"How will we do that? I suppose we could ask at reception," said Guy, lifting up the wash jug and looking inside the bowl. "Look it all matches, the chamber pot, the jug and the bowl, they are all white with blue flowers on."

Angel smiled. "Mine's exactly the same as yours. Anyway, let's go and see what we can find out."

"My door has a key, does yours?" asked Guy. "Your bag needs locking away; I wouldn't want anyone looking in there and seeing my running gear and phone."

"Anyone looking in wouldn't see anything that is not from 1913."

"That's clever," said Guy shaking his head in awe. "Everything is taken care of then."

"Yes it is, isn't it," said Angel with a wry smile.

*

"We have a question, Mr Pullum," said Guy to the man on the reception desk.

"You are staff now, call me Ted. Ask away."

"A friend of my family was in service a couple of years ago, to a lady called Elizabeth Towers, she lived in Westminster I believe, she has sadly died now, but I wondered if you knew her and if any family are still in London?"

"I knew Elizabeth and Charles Towers well; they dined here often before he died. Elizabeth occasionally dined here after his death, but I think she had mobility problems in the end. We rarely saw her the last couple of years of her life," said Ted with a kind smile. "They did live in Westminster, but I would not know where. Although the family would have sold the house by now, Elizabeth and Charles had no children of their own."

"Thank you so much for your help," said Angel. "Do you know anything about the family that inherited the house?"

"Not really, only that Elizabeth once said her

remaining family were in Manchester, other than that I have no idea."

"Also Ted, do you know a waiter called Ottomar?" asked Guy.

"We have about six waiters called Ottomar; can you narrow it down at all?" said Ted.

"Yes, he has a wife called Beatrice and children called Claude and Beattie," said Guy hopefully.

"Ah, Ottomar Waibel, yes know him well, a real gentleman. If you want to talk to him then you are out of luck, he was telling me yesterday that as it is his half day, he is taking his family to London Zoo.

"Actually," continued Ted, "Ottomar's wife used to work for the Towers family before they married. I think they met here when the Towers had come to lunch one day."

"Thank you so much, what a small world," said Guy. "Anyway, we had better leave you to get on with your work."

"It was no trouble at all to talk to you, good luck tomorrow," replied Ted.

*

The revolving door took Guy and Angel back to Northumberland Avenue which was busy with early afternoon traffic. Carts laden with sacks and churns went one way, passing carriages and cars going the other.

"They still remind me of tractors, with their big wheels and long bonnets, big head lamps and grills at the front." Guy was mesmerised by the traffic. "Mark would love it, he's car obsessed."

"Well Guy, I would say the cars have more character than the modern-day ones," said Angel as she admired a particularly large blue car passing by.

Most cars had their rooves up, due to the late October cold air, although the passengers and the driver were still exposed to the weather as the sides were not enclosed.

"It's no wonder they have blankets over their legs though, it must be freezing," Angel shivered to emphasise her point.

Some cars had a row of seats behind the driver and some didn't. Some cars also had a spare wheel attached to the side and others carried the spare wheel at the back. The cars shared the road with delivery vans, displaying the names of their companies boldly on the side as they went on their rounds. Bicycles weaved their way along Northumberland Avenue, both men and women cycled, upright and concentrating so that they didn't get hit by a car or a horse.

"I wouldn't fancy cycling round London, with all these horses and cars," said Guy. "Mind you, I wouldn't cycle round London in the twenty-first century either."

Angel grabbed Guy's arm and pointed to something. "Guy, is that…?"

"I think it is, what else could it be?" replied Guy, staring open mouthed at the cart coming towards them that was being pulled by a zebra.

"I can't believe what I'm seeing," said Guy, as the zebra passed them. The man driving the cart raised his bowler hat and smiled at Guy and Angel as he made his way up to Trafalgar Square.

"What next? Elephant rides down The Mall," laughed Guy. "Well, I'd say that's a sign, we need to go to London Zoo, it will annoy me, how small the cages are and how sad the animals' existence is, but we need to go, we might see Ottomar and Beatrice."

"A zoo, where animals from across the world are put on display for people to see, I've read about these," said Angel.

"Zoos can be quite a controversial subject in my day, some are better than others and some do quite a lot of conservation work, but that is definitely not always the case. We also have safari parks, where you drive round, the animals roam quite freely in their zones and then chase your car. Monkeys quite often take your windscreen wipers and run off with them," said Guy remembering a trip to the safari park.

"Sounds a bit scary. Where is London Zoo, do you know?" asked Angel.

"I do, it's in Regent's Park," replied Guy.

"Bus," they both said together and began walking up to Trafalgar Square.

*

"The dad was a banker and not really interested in his children's lives," said Guy explaining the plot of *Mary Poppins* to Angel, whilst they were sat on the top of a bus going to Regent's Park. "And the mum, well she was a suffragette, so she was more concerned with campaigning for women to get the vote."

"A good cause though," said Angel. "I mean, all adults should get to vote to choose their government and I know that across the world, in the present day, this doesn't always happen."

"It was a good cause, although some people would say the mum was campaigning with the wrong group," said Guy pausing to look at Oxford Circus as they made their way up Regent's Street.

"Go on," said Angel.

"Some of the buildings look the same, with their pointy rooflines and little turrets," said Guy in amazement.

"I meant about the suffragettes, I didn't realise there were other groups," said Angel following Guy's gaze down Oxford Street.

"Oh yes, well the suffragettes were only a small group of women campaigning for the vote. They were quite outrageous in their campaign tactics, not just chaining themselves to railings, they had an arson campaign, setting fire to letter boxes, golf clubhouses and even sending bombs politicians' homes," said Guy, racking his brains to remember the content of the GCSE in History he took back in June.

"What? No way!" said Angel wide eyed. "I read about them chaining themselves to railings, I didn't realise their stunts were violent too."

"Oh yes, although I don't think anyone was in when they did it, well no one got hurt as I recall. Then one suffragette threw herself in front of the King's horse at the Epsom Derby, she was killed."

"Wow, what she just ran out in front of it? I do remember something about that from our time travel lectures."

"Yeah, Emily Wilding-Davison, she was actually trying to pin something on the horse, we saw a video about it at school. She misjudged the speed of the situation and died a few days later in hospital," said Guy turning to face Angel. "Anyway, as I was saying, the suffragettes were only a small group of women campaigning for the vote, but they were the loudest. Thousands of other women campaigned more peacefully, writing letters, meeting MPs, handing out leaflets and having peaceful marches. They were led by Millicent Fawcett."

"She must have been frustrated by the suffragettes' tactics then?" said Angel thoughtfully.

"Oh yes definitely, but it is Millicent Fawcett who has a statue in Parliament Square now, my mum took us to see it the other week when we were in London for Mark's birthday."

"When you went to see *The Lion King*?" said Angel.

"Yes, that's right, mum is well into her history and she knows Mark and I like it too, he is doing a History GCSE now. The statue is quite interesting for a statue actually," said Guy.

"Why because it is a woman?" asked Angel.

"Well partly, yes, but on the plinth at the base of Millicent Fawcett are lots of little photos of other women that fought to get the vote."

"Are the suffragettes on there?" asked Angel.

"Yes, there is a photo of Emmeline Pankhurst and her three daughters."

"And yet I suspect it is the suffragettes that are remembered the most," said Angel.

"You're right there," replied Guy.

*

Guy and Angel walked through Regent's Park towards the entrance for London Zoo, Guy kicked a pile of leaves on the path and thought of his morning runs down to the lake near his house.

"It would be great to run through the London parks," said Guy.

"I don't think so Guy, we don't want you being kidnapped again," Angel grabbed Guy's arm. "You are staying right by my side this time."

Guy smiled. "I promise I will."

When they arrived at the South Entrance gate to London Zoo, they went up to the kiosk to get their tickets and were given a map of the layout.

"I hope this won't be too awful for the animals," said Guy, taking a deep breath.

They went through the gate and found themselves looking at the deer enclosure, from here they wandered round to the reptile house, not the one Guy remembered from a previous visit, but a much smaller version. All the while Guy and Angel were looking for a family that resembled Ottomar's.

They reached the Lion House and Guy winced at the small enclosures for each of the beautiful cats. Small children were being lifted up to see the big cats behind the black bars, but none of the families seemed to have a boy of five, a girl of two and a German dad.

From the Lion House they wandered past some antelope and found themselves at the Great Lawn, Guy stood aghast at the view before him. Elephants were being walked up and down the path giving rides to hordes of excited children. The majestic animals were wearing a red cover on their backs, topped with a large seat, which was big enough to fit four children each side. The keepers in their navy-blue uniforms were leading the animals up and down, whilst the children laughed and waved to people watching them.

"London Zoo has changed for the best, I don't even think it has elephants now, let alone letting people ride them," said Guy, scanning the crowd to see if he could find Ottomar.

"It does seem a bit of a sad use of these beautiful creatures," said Angel.

"Look over there," said Guy, "that family are a possibility."

Angel followed Guy's gaze and saw a family queuing up by the ladders for an elephant ride. and nodded. They moved close enough to hear a conversation, but the dad's accent was definitely not German, it was a posh English voice they heard talking to his wife.

From the great lawn they headed past the bandstand, where a brass band was playing a jaunty tune, towards the Llama House with its large clock on the top.

"I think the zoo will shut soon," said Guy. "I didn't realise it was half past four already. Oh well let's keep looking, although I don't know what we will actually say to Ottomar and Beatrice if we find them."

"It will be nice to see the whole family if nothing else. Just for context," said Angel.

They walked through a tunnel and along path where they saw parrots and the Elephant and Rhino House. They also saw a keeper leading a camel with two children on its back. When they came to an exit Guy and Angel looked at each other and nodded in agreement to follow the crowd and leave.

They walked through Regent's Park and caught a bus back to the Strand.

"I'm starving," said Angel.

"Me too," said Guy. "Where shall we eat?"

They found a little café, went in, sat down and ordered Irish stew followed by apple pie and custard.

"Not a bad day's progress," said Angel. "We have jobs in Ottomar's hotel, we know Ted on reception, and we know the Towers family are probably based in Manchester."

"We have six days to locate Ottomar's house, so that we can be in position and follow the thieves as they run away. What am I saying? We must be mad?" said Guy.

Guy and Angel laughed as their stew arrived and they began to tuck in.

Chapter 5 – Saturday 25th October 1913

Guy's alarm clock went off at seven thirty, he awoke not quite sure of his surroundings for a minute and then the enormity of the fact he was in 1913 and about to work a twelve-hour shift, came flooding back to him. He put his lamp on, pleased the hotel was fully lit by electricity and looked bleary eyed around him. Reluctantly he got out bed and straightened the bed clothes.

The water he poured into the china bowl from the matching jug, was cold and so was the room, Guy shivered and was glad to get dressed and leave his little room. He made his way down to Miss Liddington's office as she had requested and was about to knock on the door when it opened and the lady herself came out.

"Good timing Mr Devereux, well done. Now if you would like to follow me, I will take you to the kitchen," said Miss Liddington leading the way swiftly along the corridor.

They went down some stairs, along another corridor and Guy found himself in a staff locker room.

"This will be your locker. Inside you will find your kitchen uniform. Once you are changed, wash your hands and go through that door over there to the kitchen," instructed Miss Liddington. "I will meet you in there."

Guy could hear the unmistakeable clatter and clanging of a working kitchen beyond the door. He did as instructed, putting on the kitchen uniform of black trousers, a white tunic and a white mop cap, then met Miss Liddington in the kitchen. She introduced to him to a short, bald and fierce looking Mr Young, who gave him further instructions for the day.

"From eight o'clock until ten thirty you will be washing up the breakfast plates and cutlery over there," said Mr Young pointing to a sink with an already huge pile of breakfast plates waiting to be cleaned.

"Then you have a twenty-minute break, you can go next door to the staff dining room and eat your breakfast. When you come back you will go to that sink there and wash up any pans that are stacked. At one o'clock you have lunch for an hour. From two o'clock you are washing up lunch plates. At five o'clock you have a twenty-minute break again. Then you work until eight o'clock. Is that all clear?"

"Yes," said Guy with some trepidation about the day ahead.

"Remember Mr Devereux, you are on a week's trial, so work hard," added Miss Liddington.

"I will, thank you," said Guy hoping that the kitchen marathon was going to be worth it and they would be able to track the thieves, retrieve the egg and take it back to Barbara and her family.

*

Guy kept an eye on the clock in the kitchen, as he washed plate after plate and stacked them on the wire rack provided. Then he turned his attention to cutlery, used the kettle to add hot water and began by scrubbing the knives. When the cutlery was done, more plates had been delivered from breakfast. Guy scraped the breakfast plates free from leftover food and continued to wash them clean. Mr Young came over, inspected the plates and gave some back to Guy to be done again, pointing out bits he had missed.

As ten thirty approached his stomach was rumbling and Guy hoped there would be staff food in the dining room and he wasn't expected to bring breakfast. Guy looked at his hands that were now red and wrinkled from the hot water, as though he had spent too long in a hot bath. He shook his head, before plunging them back into the murky sink.

At ten thirty precisely he dried his hands and went next door. He found a huge table with bread, cheese, ham, teapots and coffee. He gathered a plate of food and a coffee and sat down next to some of the other kitchen staff.

"Hello, I'm Guy," he said to a young man whom he felt was about the same age as him.

"Stephen," said the man. "What brings you here?"

"I'm travelling with my friend; she is working as a chambermaid upstairs somewhere."

"Where are you travelling to?"

"Not sure to be honest, we worked on a farm in Essex recently, bringing in the harvest, but that's finished now, so we moved on. We will just see what happens. Although we are looking for someone who works here," said Guy. "Ottomar Waibel, he is a waiter."

"A German waiter," sneered an older man from across the table. "Too many of 'em. Working longer hours for less money. Probably all spies anyway, listening to the conversations upstairs in the restaurant, passing information back to the Kaiser."

Guy hadn't expected the anti-German sentiment in 1913, he knew the First World War started in the summer of 1914, but it seemed that tensions were rising even now.

"They probably hear secrets about our Dreadnought ships and our army. It'll all be passed back; you mark my words." The man got up and took his plate to the sink and left it.

"Bob never washes his plate up," said Stephen. "He is just sore because he wants to be a waiter, not chop vegetables, but truth is Miss Liddington won't train him because he is lazy and moans all day. The German waiters come to England fully trained, it's very organised over there.

"Anyway, I don't particularly know the waiter you mean, I haven't been here long, but I will ask around."

"Thank you, Stephen, I appreciate that," said Guy.

Stephen and Guy finished their breakfast, washed their plates and reluctantly washed Bob's breakfast things too. Then made their way back to the kitchen.

*

By one o'clock Guy's arms were aching from scrubbing pots and pans used to cook lunch, gratefully he changed out of his uniform and back into his clothes. He went up the staff stairs and saw an exit sign, needing the fresh air he went outside and found Angel waiting for him in a little staff courtyard.

"Good morning was it?" asked Angel.

"Exhausting, scrubbing pots and pans is just as hard as swinging a scythe as it turns out," said Guy rubbing his arms. "You?"

"I never want to change another bed ever," said Angel rolling her eyes. "Come on, let's get lunch somewhere and swap stories."

Guy and Angel left the courtyard through a little alleyway and made their way back to the little café in the Strand, this time they ordered chicken soup, which was cheap and very filling.

"I don't suppose you saw the suffragettes this morning, did you?" said Angel between mouthfuls, as she broke off some bread.

"I was in a basement kitchen, so no," said Guy laughing. "What were they doing?"

"There was a big group walking down Northumberland Avenue towards Trafalgar Square," said Angel.

"Were they definitely suffragettes?" asked Guy.

"Yes, Jenny, who was changing the beds with me, said they were because they had WSPU signs and they were wearing green, purple and white sashes." Angel dipped the bread in her soup and took a mouthful.

"Women's Social and Political Union," said Guy, as he too broke off some bread from the large slices they had been given.

"Jenny thought they were brilliant, she said she would love to be a suffragette, but her long shifts at the hotel don't allow her to go the meetings," said Angel, poising her spoon ready for the next mouthful. "Then Miss Liddington came in to check on things, when she looked out of the window, she shook her head and said they were silly women?"

"Well, like I said, not everyone was a fan of the Pankhurst family and the suffragettes," said Guy, dabbing his mouth with the serviette.

"Miss Liddington said whilst she agreed with the idea of votes for women, after all as she said pays her taxes, she felt that their violent tactics were going too far. She was worried that men would think women are hysterical."

"A lot of people shared her concerns, including the MPs who were on the side of giving women the vote," said Guy, getting the last spoonful of his soup ready.

"What happened in the end? Who was right?"

"Well, when World War One broke out, the suffragettes called off their tactics and supported the war effort. Then after the war there was a vote reform and in 1918 some women got the vote," said Guy.

"So, the war gave everyone a breathing space then," said Angel. "In terms of women getting the vote anyway."

"That's about it, yes. Talking about the war; there is a bit of anti-German feeling already," said Guy.

"Yes, I got that idea too," said Angel. "One of the chambermaids is dating one of the German waiters, some of the other chambermaids are quite upset by that. They called Elsie some quite unpleasant names to her face."

"I wonder what abuse Beatrice and Ottomar are getting then, that's sad," said Guy, shaking his head.

"Did you get anywhere with finding Ottomar?" asked Angel.

"No, but one of the other kitchen hands is going to ask for me. The waiters seem to use the same staff dining room as us, but I didn't meet anyone German. Mind you I was only in there for twenty minutes; they like to get their money's worth out of us don't they!"

Guy and Angel left the café and made their way back to the hotel. They stopped at the reception desk to ask Ted if he had any news on Ottomar, but Ted was on his lunch break. So, they made their way back to their respective locker rooms and prepared for an afternoon of work."

*

By five o'clock Guy was very glad of the break from washing up the lunch plates and cutlery. Putting everything away had taken ages as he had to keep asking Stephen where everything went, moreover his hands were becoming quite sore with constant soaking in hot water. He went into the staff dining room hoping to talk to some waiters, but there were none there. Guy made himself a coffee and cut a slice of fruitcake, he gladly took a seat and Stephen joined him.

"What are your plans Stephen?" asked Guy. "Do you want to be a waiter?"

"No, a chef, I'd like to save up enough money to go to France when I'm eighteen and train in Paris," said Stephen. "I'm learning here, I know it's hard work, but I love the atmosphere in the kitchen."

"How old are you now?" asked Guy.

"Sixteen," said Stephen,

"Snap," said Guy, forcing a smile. He knew only too well that in two years' time Stephen would indeed be in France, but not training to be a chef, he would be in the infamous World War One trenches, fighting against the German waiters currently employed in London. Guy hoped that Stephen's outcome would be better than

Ottomar's, as he remembered what Barbara had said, Ottomar died on the Somme battlefield in France in 1916.

"What's your surname by the way?" asked Guy, making a vow to himself to look Stephen up on the Internet when he returned home.

"Dracott," said Stephen. "Youngest son of Ellen and John Dracott from Shoreditch. I have two older brothers and three older sisters."

"Well, I'm Guy Devereux, I only have one brother, Mark, he turned fifteen last week. My dad died not long ago, I live with my mum, brother and grandparents."

"Sorry about your dad." Stephen paused before he went on. "What are your plans for work?"

"Honestly, I'd love to be a sports teacher," said Guy, "but maybe that is a dream too far."

"It's good to have a dream," said Stephen, "Who knows where we will be by 1920."

Guy nodded, he sincerely hoped Stephen became an army chef, then that way he might get through the war alive and finally find himself training in Paris.

"Back to work for the last shift then," said Guy, standing to wash his cup and plate up. "It's a long old day down in this basement."

"You get used to it. There are worse places

to be, I'd hate to be a miner or work on ship out at sea," said Stephen washing his plate up.

"There are definitely worse places to be, for sure," said Guy, unable to look Stephen in the eye.

*

At eight o'clock Guy went back to the locker room and changed, then dragged himself back up to his little room, walking through the women's corridor on his way. He noticed Angel's door was shut and that she must have already gone to bed. He went into his room and was almost too tired to undress and get into bed. Within seconds Guy was sound asleep, the clanging of the kitchen still ringing in his ears and his alarm clock set for the morning.

Chapter 6 – Sunday 26th October 1913

Once again Angel was waiting for Guy at lunchtime in the little staff courtyard, she was chatting to girl about the same age.

"Ah Guy, this is Jenny. Jenny meet Guy," said Angel introducing them to each other.

Guy went to shake Jenny's hand but stopped as he noticed her right hand and lower arm were missing, he paused feeling awkward, but Jenny put out her left hand instead.

"Lost it in a cotton mill," said Jenny, her Manchester accent very evident. "I'm used to it now though, doesn't stop me making beds and cleaning rooms, does it Angel?"

"Not at all, Jenny is the most efficient chambermaid of everyone," said Angel in admiration.

"Nice to meet you Guy, Angel talks about you a lot. Anyway, I'm off to meet me mam for a wander down the Strand, she works in a shop there. Have a nice lunch," said Jenny walking briskly across the courtyard to the alleyway.

As they walked up to Trafalgar Square, they swapped stories of their work that morning and couldn't decide whose arms were aching the most.

"Any news on Ottomar?" asked Angel.

"None at all," said Guy. "I mean Ted said he worked here, but how on earth we are going to bump into him, I have no idea. Unless he is in the little staff dining room during my breaktime, I have no hope."

"Me neither, I'm always miles away from the restaurant, there is no chance of getting down there," said Angel. "I will try my best and get in there when I finish work at six this evening."

"That sounds like a good plan, but have you seen how big the dining room is and how many waiters there are," said Guy as they reached Trafalgar Square.

"It is a very busy place isn't it, but he must be there, luckily it's still only Sunday, so we have all week to work it out," said Angel, linking her arm through Guy's. "Where should we eat? Same place?"

Guy nodded and they made their way into the Strand and headed towards their favourite little café.

*

When they arrived back at the Hotel Victoria, Guy and Angel were amazed to see a red carpet laid out from the road and up the steps into the foyer of the hotel. Intrigued, they decided to ask Ted what was going on and went to find him.

"Hello Ted," said Angel. "What is the red carpet all about?"

"Ah, we have some very important people coming for dinner tonight," said Ted, standing taller and raising his head. "None other than His Majesty, King George V and his wife Queen Mary. They will be arriving about six o'clock for dinner and they will be joined by the Prime Minister, Mr Asquith and his wife. It is a great honour that they often to choose our hotel to have Sunday dinner."

"That is an honour indeed, isn't it," said Angel. "The chefs must have a good reputation."

"So, I will be washing up the King and Queen's plate then," laughed Guy.

"Not everyone can say they have done that," said Angel rubbing Guy's aching arm.

"I don't suppose you spoke to Ottomar did you?" asked Guy.

"I haven't seen him no. I think the waiters are very busy today, not only with Sunday lunch, but with the royal visit. If I do seem him though, I will tell him to go down to the kitchen and find you."

"Thank you so much for your help," said Guy. "Say hello to the King for me."

"Oh well back to work then," said Angel. "Bye Ted, see you later Guy."

*

Guy and Angel met back in the staff courtyard at ten past eight that evening.

"I'm so sorry Guy, the restaurant is out of bounds what with the royal party. I had no chance of getting in to find Ottomar," said Angel.

"I really didn't think it would be that difficult to find him," sighed Guy. "Oh well, like you said, it's Sunday and theft takes place on Friday, we still have plenty of time."

"Shall we go and find something to eat and maybe go for a walk?" said Angel.

"Always ready to eat," said Guy.

*

Guy and Angel wandered along The Mall towards Buckingham Palace, they were on the edge of St. James' Park, the occasional streetlamp lighting the way. The Mall was quite empty, but then it was a cold October evening. They were engrossed in their conversation, confirming everything they knew so far, and playing out different scenarios after the theft and how they might retrieve the Faberge egg.

Suddenly a woman appeared from across the road, she was running and was clearly struggling to carry on as she was out of breath.

"Don't tell on me, please don't tell on me," she said to Guy and Angel between gasps. "I cannot go back to prison, I just can't, I'm exhausted." With that she disappeared into some bushes in St. James' Park.

Guy and Angel stared at the bushes and then at one another.

"I think I know what this is," said Guy, "Did you see the purple and green sash under her coat? She's a suffragette, I'm sure of it."

"Well, you would know, I'm sure you are right," agreed Angel.

"I remember this from GCSE History, it's the Cat and Mouse Act. When the suffragettes got sent to prison, they wanted to be treated as political prisoners and not common criminals, but the authorities refused their demands. The women then went on hunger strike, so the prison guards force fed them, but this led to bad publicity. So, the government came up with the idea of releasing the women when they were getting weak due to not eating and then re-arresting them a few weeks later and taking them back to prison to finish their sentence. It was brutal."

Just as Guy finished his explanation, two police officers came running across the road.

"Did you see a woman come this way?" asked one of the police officers.

"Yes officer, we did," replied Angel. "There was a motor car waiting for her, she's gone."

"Bloody Pankhurst's, they've picked her up again. She's given us the slip," said one of the policemen.

"Don't worry, she can't hide forever," said the other. "Thank you, mam, sir." With that the police officers retreated the way they had come.

Guy and Angel stayed to check the woman was alright, after a few minutes the exhausted suffragette emerged from the bushes and thanked Guy and Angel. "Let me repay your kindness, come and have supper at the safe house with me; Mrs Pankhurst would be delighted to thank you," she said as a car pulled up.

"No, we couldn't possibly," said Angel, "but you're very kind to offer."

The suffragette walked to the car and spoke to the driver who got out to open the door for her.

"Wait, wait," said Guy to Angel, "I think we should go. The Pankhurst's are from Manchester, and so are the Towers, this could be useful."

"I'm so glad you listened in History lessons," whispered Angel. Then added to the suffragette, "we'd love to come actually, thank you."

*

Once in the car with the suffragette, she introduced herself formally as Miss Sarah Clarke and they drove off towards Buckingham Palace. After a few twists and turns, the car pulled up outside a house and the little party went inside. Guy and Angel were shown into small room by Sarah and told to wait. After a couple of minutes, the door opened, a woman came in with Sarah in tow. Guy recognised the woman at once from the many photos in history books.

"I am Mrs Pankhurst, pleased to meet you. I really cannot thank you enough. Poor Miss Clarke has been re-arrested twice now; I fear for her health if she were to spend another day in prison, let alone a week. This so-called Cat and Mouse Act is horrific." Mrs Pankhurst shook their hands. "What are your names?"

"I'm Miss Jasmine and this is Mr Devereux," said Angel.

"I'm so very pleased to meet you," said Guy, a little starstruck.

"Miss Jasmine are you part of the suffrage movement? We need as many young women as possible to join our cause."

"I have only just arrived in London, but the cause interests me greatly," said Angel. "Perhaps I could come to a meeting sometime soon."

"Yes, you must, indeed, I will give you some details," said Mrs Pankhurst. "Now let's have supper, there is plenty to go round, and I will of course arrange for the car to take you home."

"You are very kind Mrs Pankhurst," said Angel.

"Not at all, you saved Miss Clarke from prison, she is far too exhausted to go back so soon.

*

"The funeral procession was enormous, and so solemn. It was such a tribute to Emily Wilding Davison, after all she gave her life for the cause," said Mrs Pankhurst, as they sat around the table enjoying steak and kidney pudding, potatoes and carrots.

"Do you think she meant to die that day?" asked Guy.

"She had bought a return ticket to Epsom Racecourse, that tells me that she expected to return home. However, she knew that running out in front of the King's horse was dangerous and I think she was prepared to put her life at risk. So brave," Mrs Pankhurst turned to smile at Sarah.

"I heard she was trying to pin a suffragette banner on the horse," said Guy.

"I believe so, that might be the case, but nothing was ever found," said Mrs Pankhurst.

Guy nodded and ate some of his supper, he

knew full well that the banner would turn up years later, a policeman had taken it from the scene, it was in the video he watched at school.

"What was prison like? If you don't mind me asking," said Angel to Sarah.

"The force feeding is the worst, wardresses pinning you down and the more they force feed you, the more painful it becomes, so you resist," Sarah paused.

Mrs Pankhurst continued. "When the wardresses pin you down, they injure your legs, or your ribs with their full weight. They care not if your head bangs against the wall, but it is the tube going up your nose that causes the most pain."

"They just push and push, it's excruciating," Sarah put a hand to her throat and closed her eyes.

Mrs Pankhurst continued once more. "It's the brutality with which they administer the tube that is so degrading, they care not for your pain, indeed they make it as painful as possible, digging their nails into your face to add to the humiliation."

"You are left bruised and swollen from the continual forced feeding and when your nose cannot take anymore, they use a throat tube." Sarah shuddered at the memory and Mrs Pankhurst put a hand on her arm. "And now we play cat and mouse, I cannot thank you enough for not giving me away."

Guy and Angel had stopped eating as they sat in listened in awe to the two suffragettes, who were prepared to suffer so much for their cause.

"Thank you for sharing your experiences with us," said Angel. "It cannot be easy and yet you carry on regardless."

"We shall carry on until women have the vote, that you can count on," said Mrs Pankhurst.

*

Shaking hands with the suffragettes, Guy and Angel prepared to leave, thanking them for their hospitality.

"Miss Jasmine, here is our newspaper for you and here is the address of a meeting house, not too far from Trafalgar Square. Perhaps you could join us at our next rally," said Mrs Pankhurst. "I won't be at the meeting myself this week; I am heading back to Manchester to draw up some support from that area. We have a big reception next Sunday afternoon at Manchester Town Hall."

"I will do my best to attend a meeting," said Angel smiling. "It is not acceptable that women cannot vote."

With that Angel and Guy left the house and got back into the waiting car.

*

"Angel, you cannot go off and be a suffragette," Guy said, grabbing Angel's arm as they walked back into the Hotel Victoria after the car had dropped them off. "If you get arrested and sent to prison, what then?"

"Don't panic, I was just being polite, I promise we will stick together this time," said Angel trying to reassure Guy. "I have no intention of going to prison, no matter how worthy the cause, we have a job to do."

"We need to find Ottomar, I really thought we would have found him by now, it's so frustrating," said Guy, leading the way up the staff stairs.

"There's still plenty of time," said Angel, stifling a yawn, "and I promise I do not want to be in this situation." Angel pointed to the front page of the newspaper that Mrs Pankhurst had given her. It showed a suffragette being led away, with the headline *The Brutal Arrest of Miss Annie Kenney.*

Chapter 7 – Monday 27th October 1913

Guy enjoyed not having to wake up with the alarm clock on Monday morning, the long hotel shifts were exhausting and he slept in until nine o'clock. He had just finished getting dressed when there was a knock at his door.

"Come in," he said, tidying his bed.

"Sleep well?" inquired Angel.

"Very. You?

"Absolutely. Now we need to get down to the waiter area and track down the elusive Ottomar," said Angel. "He has to be there today."

*

"I'm so sorry," said Ted. "I did tell him last night that there were two people looking for him. He knows to come and look for you now, but it's his day off. Ottomar is taking his family down to Southend to walk on the long pier, it's the longest in the world, so I believe."

"Thank you, Ted, hopefully we shall catch up with him tomorrow then," said Angel. "At least we are a step nearer to meeting him.

Guy and Angel left the foyer through the revolving door and went out to Northumberland Avenue, which was already busy with delivery vans and carts, bicycles and buses, all weaving along together.

"Let's go to Southend," said Angel. "We might as well, we have the day off and you never know, we might actually spot them today."

"Ok, but if we do spot them today, I don't think we should introduce ourselves, Ottomar will think we are stalking him," said Guy with a grimace.

"Agreed," said Angel leading the way up to Trafalgar Square. "Come on, let's find a bakery and get some breakfast."

"Good idea," said Guy, "I'm starving."

*

They bought their breakfast from a little bakery on Trafalgar Square and sat down on a bench by Nelson's column to eat their bacon rolls. Then they found a bus to Liverpool Street station, and took their seats on the top deck, braving the crisp cold air.

The bus trundled back down the Strand, through Holborn and Fleet Street, round St. Paul's

Cathedral, down Cheapside and along to Liverpool Street station. Guy and Angel entered the station down a set of steep stairs and went to the ticket booths. Tickets purchased, they found a train to Southend and boarded listening as the train whistled and puffed ready to depart. It wasn't long before they were chugging towards the coast and the seaside town of Southend.

"What are we actually going to say to Ottomar? Not today, I mean when we talk to him at the hotel." said Guy. "We haven't really discussed that."

"We need to be very careful," said Angel. "We cannot say anything that alerts him to the theft of the Faberge egg, likewise we cannot alert him to his fate in the war at any cost."

"I seem to make a habit of meeting doomed men, Charles I, Father Thomason and now Ottomar," said Guy sadly.

"Think about little Chloe and her operation, that's the reason we are here," said Angel, laying a hand on Guy's arm. "It's all about the present day now, this has already happened, we cannot change that."

Guy nodded and looked out of the window as the steam blew past, blocking his view of the Essex countryside. Time travel was an emotional journey, as well as being physically very difficult.

"I think we could say to Ottomar, that we

bumped into Beatrice's Aunt Mary recently, surely everyone has an Aunt Mary in 1913, and that she has given us some presents for the children," said Angel. "What do you think?"

Guy looked open mouthed at Angel.

"It might work, don't look so shocked Guy. We could get a little present for each of the children." Angel looked very pleased with herself. "I believe teddy bears are the toy of the moment, aren't they? I'm sure I read that somewhere."

"I suppose so, I don't know. What if Beatrice doesn't have an Aunt Mary though?"

"I will make something up, don't worry. Let's get a couple of teddy bears today anyway, I think this could work."

"Ok, it's all we've got, so let's go for it. Teddy bear shopping in Southend it is." Guy shook his head. "I'm not sure they have teddy bears in 1913 though."

"It was something to do with the American president, Teddy Roosevelt, but I can't remember the whole story," said Angel, taking her turn to share some historic facts.

*

The train pulled into Southend-on-Sea station, Guy and Angel stood up ready to leave the carriage.

"I'm sure this station is called Southend

Victoria now," said Guy. Anyway, it is a short walk through the High Street to the seafront and then the pier."

"We can look for teddy bears then," said Angel grinning, still pleased with her idea.

They left the station and wandered through the High Street, looking under the candy-striped canopies into the shop windows, scouring the goods for teddy bears. They spotted a toy shop and had a quick look in.

"Perfect," said Angel. "Let's buy them on the way back.

"Good old Aunt Mary," said Guy rolling his eyes.

*

As they made their way down to the seafront Guy and Angel pointed out families that might be Ottomar and Beatrice, but none of the dads turned out to be German.

"Walk or ride the train? It's a mile long this pier," said Guy proudly.

"Can we walk one way and ride the other?" asked Angel.

"Yes, good idea, let's walk out and ride back, that's what most people do."

Whilst it wasn't a terribly cold day in Southend, the further Guy and Angel got down the pier, the windier it became.

"You really have to concentrate on the boardwalk don't you," declared Angel, trying not to trip on the gaps between the planks. "Also, these railings are not that high, I'm slightly worried I will be blown over the side."

"Don't worry, I'm good swimmer, I will save you," said Guy.

Angel rolled her eyes. "Thanks, but I will fly to shore, I'm good in the wind."

Guy stopped and paused for a moment. "Wait, you can fly?"

"Well let's hope you don't have to find out," said Angel laughing.

"I feel like I don't really know you sometimes, what other hidden talents do you have?" Guy walked over to the railings and held on.

"Apart from creating time bending wind tunnels, not many really," Angel joined him and held on tightly to the railings.

"This is the longest pleasure pier in the world, even now in my day," said Guy changing the subject and looking back to the shore. "It seems funny seeing the shore without Adventure Island and all the rides there. Although the hotel on the hill is still there in the present day."

Guy and Angel pressed on to the end of the pier and took in the sea breeze.

"No sign of Ottomar and Beatrice," said Guy. "Then again, there are not many people here at all, it is a Monday in late October I suppose."

"I should think their kids would be blown away," said Angel, gripping the railings.

"It is blowy isn't it," said Guy doing likewise.

It was a relief to get out of the wind and onto the train that took Guy and Angel back to shore. Back on the sea front they made their way along the little parade of shops and caught the smell of fish and chips. A quick glance at each other and a nod, they found a fish and chip shop with spaces, went in and sat down. It was not long before they were tucking into cod and chips, with salt and vinegar.

"I needed that," said Guy. "And it tastes exactly the same in the present day. Compulsory seaside food."

"It's very tasty, my first fish and chips ever," said Angel.

"You haven't lived," said Guy.

"Well, no, I haven't, not in a sense that you would know anyway," said Angel smiling.

"Can you tell me more about your background?" asked Guy.

"Not really much to say, I was made a guardian angel earlier this year, but then you know that already."

"What were you before?" asked Guy, desperate for more information about his companion.

"I was in training before that," said Angel, loading her fork with fluffy white cod and two chips.

"You don't give much away do you," sighed Guy.

"Just go with the flow." Angel smiled and ate the food from her fork.

"How long does training last?" Guy pushed for more information.

"It depends on how good you are really," said Angel taking another mouthful of cod.

Guy gave up and changed the subject. "I think we should walk down to the Kursaal."

"What's that?" asked Angel.

"In my day it's a bowling alley, but I think it will be a funfair in 1913."

"Sounds good, I have read about funfairs, it would be great to see one. Will there be rides?"

"I think so, I'm not sure, the Kursaal has changed a lot over the years," said Guy, finishing the last chip.

*

Guy was quite surprised to see that Kursaal funfair, was in fact called the Luna Park in 1913.

Smiling they went through the entrance of the domed red brick building.

"Ew, a circus," Guy pulled a face. "After the zoo I don't think I can face a circus."

"I agree," said Angel. "I wonder what else they have."

"Perhaps we can win a couple of teddy bears on a coconut shy," said Guy, winking at Angel.

"I like the sound of this Guy, *The Harton Scenic Railway*, I think we should give it a go. I read about these, they sound like fun," said Angel, as she pulled Guy towards the ride's entrance.

"To be fair I do like a wooden rollercoaster." Guy needed no encouragement to have a go on the ride.

They sat in the front of the little car and held on to the bar. The ride began and the car slowly made its way uphill, creaking and squeaking as they went. The anticipation built as they reached the top. Guy was more interested in watching Angel's reaction, than he was in the excitement of the first initial drop. The car lurched forward and began its very quick descent. Angel laughed out loud until the drop took her breath away. The car slowed as it began another climb and Angel had the biggest smile on her face, as she held onto her hat. The little car wound its way up and down around the track until it finally ground to a halt with a jolt.

"That was amazing, let's go again," said Angel, already running back to the ride entrance.

After two more goes, Angel finally decided that was enough.

"Thank goodness," said Guy. "I thought I was going to see my fish and chips again if went round once more." Guy laughed. "Perhaps the carousel will be a good next ride to try."

"Oh yes, let's do that," Angel grabbed Guy's arm and led him towards the golden horses.

They paid their money and got on the carousel, selecting horses that were side by side. Guy thought it was lovely to see Angel laugh and enjoy herself, she was usually focused and sensible, thinking about their next move. He did however laugh as she tried to get on the carousel in her long navy skirt. She had to be content with sitting side saddle in the end. The music started and the carousel began to move round, as the horses began to go up and down.

"Oh, this is so relaxing," said Angel, leaning against the pole and shutting her eyes.

Eventually the ride began to slow and come to a stop, they got off and looked around to see what else was available. Some of the rides seemed to be closed, but there was indeed a coconut shy, however the prizes were not teddy bears but sticks of Southend rock and toffee apples.

"They will break your teeth and I don't fancy a 1913 visit to the dentist," said Guy pulling Angel away.

Having fully explored the funfair, and settling for doughnuts not rock, Guy and Angel made their way back along the seafront, up the hill and back to the High Street. They found the teddy bear shop and bought two little light brown teddy bears for Claude and Beattie, in the hope that they would meet them one day soon and then they made their way back to the station.

"My first visit to the seaside," said Angel. "We didn't find Ottomar and Beatrice, but it's all good research for me. Not a day is wasted during time travel, that is what they said during training."

"Who are they?" asked Guy.

"The time travel trainers," replied Angel shrugging her shoulders. "They said we should embrace all experiences, especially new ones because we never know when we might need them."

"They are very wise," said Guy, opening the door for Angel to get on the train as the steam rose in fluffy white clouds above their heads.

Chapter 8 – Tuesday 28th October 1913

A loud clattering clang made Guy jump and he splashed water all over the floor.

"That is it, enough!" yelled Mr Young at Bob. "I have had enough of you and your butter fingers. All of that veg will need to be thrown and prepared again, as it is now rolling around the floor."

Bob turned to face Mr Young, blood dripping from his hand.

"I care not that you have cut yourself, again! Get out! Go and see Miss Liddington, you're fired!"

"But…" began Bob.

"No buts – get out. Guy, clear this mess up and start preparing the veg, Stephen will show you what to do."

"Mr Young, please, I need this job…" said Bob, his eyes misty.

"If you needed it, you would do it properly, you don't pull your weight and you make too many mistakes, go and work in a café, you're not fit for this hotel. Go!"

Bob reluctantly turned towards the door and sloped out, Guy felt sorry for him and now he would have to prepare vegetables. He watched Stephen whose hands moved like lightening, let out a sigh and went to find a dustpan and brush to clear up Bob's mess.

*

"What a long morning," said Guy rubbing his hands. "I could really do with some hand cream; can you get *trench hands*?"

"I'm sure we can look for some handcream," said Angel taking Guy's hands in hers and looking at them. "They do look a bit chapped."

"I honestly don't know how people do this job for months on end," said Guy. "And now I have to prepare veg too, and there's no one else to wash up, so I'm doing mine and Bob's job. Although to be fair Stephen is also doing Bob's job."

"Don't go chopping a finger off or anything, that is a complication I don't need."

"No! Neither do I." Guy laughed and scrunched his hands up as if to protect them.

The door opened and a waiter emerged looking round to see who was outside.

"Are you Mr Devereux and Miss Jasmine?" said the man in an unmistakable German accent.

"Yes, are you Mr Waibel?" replied Angel hopefully.

"I am indeed."

"We are so pleased to meet you," said Angel, shaking his hand.

Guy followed suit, taking in Ottomar's sandy blond hair, blue eyes and large moustache.

"We have been looking for you, we met a relative of your wife's recently and she has given us a little present each for your children, Claude and Beattie, I believe," said Angel.

"How lovely," said Ottomar.

"Guy and I have our half day tomorrow and we are keen to see as much of London as possible whilst we are here, could we deliver the little teddies ourselves?" asked Angel, thinking quickly.

"Of course, what a lovely idea. I will write down the address for you. I won't be there but I will let Mrs Waibel, Beatrice, know you are coming. What time do you think you will arrive?"

"How long does it take to get there?" asked Guy.

"If you take the underground, it is quite quick, about forty minutes from here," said Ottomar. "You take a train from Charing Cross Embankment to Elephant and Castle, then change trains and go to the Oval. I will draw you a map from there, it's not complicated."

"We should be with her by three o'clock I should think," said Angel. "We won't stay long; we shall just deliver the teddy bears to the children."

"She will enjoy the company and so will the children, Beatrice does not work at the moment," said Ottomar. "It is so kind of you to deliver the teddy bears. I must get back to work, but I will get the address and map down to the kitchen later." Ottomar shook their hands again and disappeared back through the door.

"At last, progress," said Angel, as they began their walk out to the street. "We can actually find out where they live and be ready for Friday."

"Fantastic but Angel, you are a such liar. Is that ethical?" laughed Guy. "Slightly worrying how easily you pull out an untruth."

"It's for a good cause, little Chloe needs that operation in the USA, and we need to get that Faberge egg back for Barbara to sell," said Angel. "We have job to do, and we are getting closer. So, it's not lying exactly, it is telling people a version of something that makes sense to them and hides our true identity."

"The bigger picture it is then, onwards to the Oval tomorrow."

"Not before you wash some more pots and pans and prepare some more veg."

"Thank you for reminding me, I had

forgotten." Guy rolled his eyes.

Chapter 9 – Wednesday 29th October 1913

It was a rainy, dull day in London, Guy and Angel went to the bakery in Trafalgar Square and were now clutching little paper bags close to their chests. Guy was carrying the two teddy bears from the toy shop in Southend, whilst Angel had bags containing cheese rolls for their lunch. They made their way down Whitehall heading towards the Embankment station, their borrowed umbrellas straining against the wind. The tall white imposing buildings of Whitehall towered above them as they made their way towards the left turn that would take them to the station.

"Oh no, Angel, come back," called Guy.

Angel turned to look at Guy pulling a face at being asked to stop in the wind and rain, but she made her way back to him.

"Angel, this is so sad." Guy was standing in the street looking up at a window in one of the large white buildings.

"Why?" asked Angel completely confused.

"See that window on the first floor there," said Guy pointing. "I saw a video at school years ago, it's the window where Charles the First stepped through onto a huge platform and was executed."

"Oh Guy, that must be weird for you, you only met him a couple of months ago," said Angel sympathetically.

"It is actually weird, it makes me feel sad, I know he made a lot of mistakes, but to be beheaded in front of crowd, it must have been terrifying. In fact, I seem to remember that he wore two shirts because he didn't want to be seen to shiver," said Guy shivering himself in sympathy with the doomed King.

They both sighed and had a second to reflect, before continuing on their way to the station. Grateful to arrive and get out of the rain, they shook their umbrellas as they put them down. Tickets purchased they proceeded down to the Bakerloo Line to catch the train to Elephant and Castle.

"The station looks almost exactly the same, yellow and green tiles, same steps down to the platform. This is bizarre, I wonder if they are steam trains," said Guy.

"I don't think so," said Angel. "It looks like electric tracks to me."

"I think you are right," said Guy peering over the platform edge.

Within minutes the red electric train pulled in and the doors opened. Guy and Angel got on the train, which was not too packed with people, but no seats were available. Guy felt that his London Underground experience in 1913, was very similar to his twenty-first century experience so far. The doors shut and the train pulled away, in no time at all they pulled into Waterloo station, the next station was not one that Guy recognised, Westminster Bridge Road, the third stop was where they had to change trains, Elephant and Castle. As they had a ten minute wait according to the guard, they found a bench and ate their cheese rolls. Having swapped lines from the Bakerloo Line to the City and South London Line, again, not one that Guy was familiar with, they caught the south bound train. It stopped at Kennington before they alighted at the Oval station, as Ottomar had instructed them to do.

"Let's look at Ottomar's map before we leave the station, otherwise it will get soaked," said Angel looking at the rain, which had not improved since they got on at the Embankment.

"We have to walk in a v shape look, south until we come to the South Lambeth Road and then we go north to Coronation Buildings. They live at one hundred and forty-nine," said Guy. "It's not really the day for a long walk is it."

They covered the ground quickly, umbrellas protecting them from the worst of the rain and within fifteen minutes they found themselves outside Coronation Buildings. Glad to be out of the rain once more, and having located the correct stairwell, they made their way up to flat one hundred and forty-nine.

"I feel quite nervous," said Guy. "I really hope Beatrice has an Aunt Mary."

"Don't worry, I will think on my feet if she hasn't, promise," said Angel knocking on the door.

Beatrice opened the door, little Beattie in her arms and Claude hiding behind her legs.

"Hello, I'm Mrs Waibel, do call me Beatrice, come in, come and warm yourself up in front of the fire. It's so nice of you to come all this way," Beatrice took their jackets and hung them near the fire in the little kitchen. "Sit down, sit down, I will make tea. Did you find me easily enough?"

"Yes, Mr Waibel's map was very easy to follow. I'm Miss Jasmine and this is Mr Devereux," said Angel shaking Beatrice's hand. "But do call us Guy and Angel." Angel then turned to address the children. "Hello, you must Claude and you must be Beattie."

Introductions out of the way, Beatrice busied herself making tea, as Guy and Angel sat down at the little table in the kitchen and enjoyed the warmth of the fire.

"We'll let that draw a while," said Beatrice setting down the yellow teapot, decorated with pink flowers, on the table. She then added a brown knitted tea cosy and set out the cups for all three of them. Lastly, she put a Victoria sponge cake on the table, with a pile of plates and a knife and then she sat down. Upon seeing the cake, little Claude made himself comfortable in the fourth chair.

"We just wanted to visit and give your children these teddy bears in person," said Angel, poising the bag to be opened.

"Ottomar said they are from an aunt of mine?" said Beatrice, looking puzzled.

"Indeed, they are, from your Aunt Mary," said Angel, as Guy held his breath.

"That is so sweet of her, she always remembers the children. I haven't seen her for ages actually, she must be getting on now, bless her," Beatrice put her hands together in prayer and Guy let out a silent sigh of relief.

"She was well when saw her," reassured Angel, lifting the first bear from her bag and passing it to Claude, who took the bear and hugged it to him whispering a thank you. Angel handed the second bear to Beattie, who was too shy to take it. Beatrice sat Beattie on her lap and took the bear, handing it to her child, who was happy to take it from her mother, she too hugged the bear and Beatrice reminded her to say thank you, which she did, although it sounded more like Q than the actual words.

Beatrice set her daughter down, poured the tea and served the cake, Claude tucked in straight away. Beatrice picked up Beattie again and gave her a piece of cake too.

"I hear you used to work for the Towers family. One of my aunts was also in service there, Katrina Devereux," said Guy, using his mum's name because it was all he could think of. "Did you know her?"

"Oh, it's a small world isn't it, but that must have been after my time, no sorry I didn't know her," said Beatrice.

The conversation was now open for Guy to continue. "What do you know of the family now?"

"Henry Towers lives in Manchester with his wife Letitia, he runs a cotton mill, but I hear it is having financial difficulties, not that I'm bothered, he is not a nice man," said Beatrice shaking her head and shuddering. "I had some dealings with Henry Towers recently and he was so rude to my Ottomar, mostly because he is German. I think his factory is losing out to competition from Germany and with all this talk of war, well, anyway, he was quite a nasty fellow."

"He sounds awful," said Angel.

"His factory is really being kept going by

his wife's family and their money. I imagine he will lose it soon; he hasn't invested in new machinery and the Germans are becoming more efficient in their cotton production. Well, that's what Elizabeth Towers' solicitor told me anyway." Beatrice shook her head and took another mouthful of cake.

Guy and Angel did not pry, but they knew that Beatrice had spoken to Elizabeth Tower's solicitor because Henry Towers had accused her of stealing the Faberge egg.

"Can I get down please mummy?" asked Claude.

"Of course, darling," said Beatrice.

Claude and Beattie went off to play with some small toy animals that were on the floor. Guy thought the animals were probably a little souvenir from the family's trip to the zoo last Friday.

"Claude was a very brave boy last week, he climbed up a big ladder and rode on the back of an elephant, didn't you Claude, did you enjoy it?"

"It was very bouncy," said Claude, picking up a toy elephant and bouncing it along.

"That was very brave indeed," said Guy, smiling at Claude who looked very proud.

"I went on a train on the pier too, it was a very windy day," said Claude.

Guy and Angel laughed.

"You have been busy haven't you," said Angel. "You are a very lucky boy.

"Ottomar likes to spoil them, there are rumours that if we go to war Germans will be sent home. Even worse, he would have to fight for Germany." Beatrice paused and watched the children play. "Yes, I think it's very much on his mind."

"Let's hope it doesn't come to that," said Guy smiling at Beatrice, but feeling a sinking sensation in the pit of his stomach.

*

Having finished their cake and tea, Guy and Angel said their goodbyes and thanked Beatrice for her hospitality. She thanked them for coming and Guy and Angel made their way back to the station in the rain, which was now a light drizzle. The South London roads were just as busy as the West End, but here they had trams as well, adding another dynamic to anyone trying to cross from one side to the other.

As they went into Oval station Guy and Angel put down their umbrellas and were shaking them out, when a couple of young men, not looking where they were going bumped into them. The two men pushed Guy and Angel aside quite roughly and called them a couple of rude names.

"Hey, no need for that," said Guy angrily.

"Just leave it Guy, they are not worth it," said Angel pulling Guy towards to the ticket booth.

"Are you ok?" asked Guy.

"I'm fine, really, let's get back to the West End and get some of that Irish Stew for dinner," reassured Angel.

*

"Shall we walk up to Leicester Square and Piccadilly Circus? I'd quite like to see the 1913 version of these places," said Guy as they left the little café in the Strand.

"Do you know the way?" asked Angel, putting her gloves on and straightening her hat.

"I know the general direction, we can wander a bit, it's only six thirty, we've got plenty of time to kill."

"Sounds like a plan then," agreed Angel, as they crossed the Strand in between two horse drawn carts and a bus heading towards Trafalgar Square.

They walked up and crossed Charing Cross Road into Irving Street. It was now quite dark, the streetlamps flickered in the cold air, but the streets were still busy with people making their way with great purpose to their destinations. As they emerged on to Leicester Square the night sky became more illuminated with the lights from the buildings surrounding the gardens. The trees had nearly finished shedding leaves, many of which were scattered across the ground and bobbling in the light wind. The buildings looked familiar to Guy, although there was less colour than in the present day, as there were no billboards advertising various musicals.

"You're very quiet Guy," said Angel looking around. "Are you ok?"

"Yes, I'm good, I guess everything just reminds me of my dad. I remember being here with my mum and dad, and Mark of course. There is a huge *M and M* shop here in my time, we went there and bought so much chocolate, it lasted for weeks."

"Memories are good, but they can hurt too, can't they?" said Angel looking sad.

Guy turned to Angel and was about to ask a question when she changed the subject and the moment passed.

"Are there any cinemas here?" she asked.

"I don't know, I imagine there were silent movies by 1913, so maybe. Why?"

"I have read about cinemas, but obviously there weren't any in 1648, so I couldn't experience one."

"Well, a 1913 cinema will be very different from what I'm used to, that said, the building might be the same, shall we find one?" Guy said.

Looking this way and that, they walked across Leicester Square, into Coventry Street and there in front them was a building that Guy was sure he had walked past before, he was also sure it had never been lit up like it was now, he would have remembered it. The tall white stone building had a huge arched window that was framed by a bright red neon light, no other building around them was glowing in quite the way the West End Cinema was.

"I think we've found a cinema," said Angel. "You can't really miss it can you."

"It looks like *David Copperfield* is showing," said Guy looking at the poster by the door.

"That's a Charles Dickens story isn't it, I have read it." Angel looked pleased with herself.

"Wow, you've read a whole Dickens, that's impressive, I don't think I could. I have seen it though, as a play, we went on a school trip once."

"This is perfect then; we both know the story. Shall we go in, it says the next showing is seven thirty," said Angel, linking arms with Guy and steering him towards the ticket office in the foyer, which was flanked by huge ferns and palms.

Tickets purchased at two shillings each, they entered the cinema auditorium, both giving a gasp at the sheer size of the space, a central dome raising the ceiling in an already large room. Guy and Angel's tickets took them to plush red velvety seats that were towards the back of the curved balcony, giving them a fantastic view of the whole cinema.

"I think this is quite a new cinema, look how fresh everything is," said Guy pointing to the cream and gold paintwork on the dome.

"It's beautiful, just stunning," said Angel in awe of the first cinema she had ever been in. "Little touches of pink, make it feel quite cosy."

"That and the fact it is packed out, I can't see a spare seat anywhere," said Guy.

The huge screen was currently hidden, draped in a black curtain, in front of which was an orchestra pit.

"Oh, wow, it has live music, this is going to be an experience," said Guy as he craned his neck to watch the musicians taking their places and tuning up their instruments.

"It sounds like it will be very dramatic," said Angel as the lights went down and the audience noise hushed.

The curtains slid apart, and the orchestra began to play in unison, guided by the conductor at the front. The screen lit up and a *Pathe Newsreel* began to play.

The first item was about a mining disaster in

Wales, where four hundred and thirty-nine miners had died in a methane explosion. Guy and Angel looked at each other in horror as the tale was told. Images of the colliery played to sad slow music from the orchestra. Information about the disaster was given on written slides that broke up the footage of men being carried away on stretchers. The next images were horse drawn funeral carriages carrying coffins through crowded streets of mourners.

"I wasn't expecting that," said Guy, the news doesn't change, does it? So much misery."

"So sad, it said that half the breadwinners from the community were killed, how did people afford to live with no wage coming in? Horrendous," said Angel, her eyes cast downward.

The news reel moved on to a battleship being launched. The information slide said it was the *HMS Queen Elizabeth*, an oil-fired dreadnought being launched at Portsmouth Dockyard. Guy noted it was just called Queen Elizabeth, not Queen Elizabeth the First, as Queen Elizabeth the Second had not been born, let alone become queen yet.

"I remember learning about the naval race with Germany in History lessons, funny to see it here, in action," said Guy leaning over and talking quietly to Angel.

"And a sign of the horror to come," added

Angel. "I too had to learn about the First World War," she whispered.

The newsreel finished and the orchestra picked up the mood as the titles began to roll for *David Copperfield*. The next hour saw Guy and Angel spellbound by the tale of *David Copperfield*, from a child, through teenage years and onto being an adult, three actors taking on the title role. The story was told through the black and white information slides, the scenes were enhanced with the music, sometimes light and bouncy, other times slow and gloomy.

When the lights came on at the end Guy and Angel were breathless, as though they had been on a rollercoaster of emotions.

"I didn't realise silent movies could be so powerful," said Guy. "I'm impressed. What an experience, not that I will be able to tell anyone." He laughed and stood up, putting an arm out for Angel to lean on. "Back out to the cold then, are you ready?"

"I guess so, I feel quite emotional to be honest. Although I feel more emotional about changing all those beds tomorrow," said Angel rolling her eyes.

"Oh, don't remind me, back to scraping breakfast off plates and hours of washing up. I can't wait."

"Only one more day though," said Angel as

they followed the crowd out of the auditorium and down the stairs to the ferny foyer. "We shall have to leave Friday morning and get ourselves down to Lambeth."

"Definitely, don't want to miss those thieves, we have come so far now."

"When shall we tell the hotel we are going?" asked Angel, taking a deep breath in the cold night air.

"Early morning let's go to Miss Liddington's office at seven thirty on Friday morning and tell her. She will be annoyed but..." Guy paused.

"There is a bigger picture, we are here for a good purpose, and they have had good work from us this week, don't feel guilty."

"I won't," said Guy as they linked arms and headed off in the direction of Eros at Piccadilly Circus.

Chapter 10 – Thursday 30th October 1913

Miss Liddington came into the kitchen as Guy was ploughing his way through washing up the breakfast plates, knowing it was his last day at the kitchen sink. She tapped him on the back and made him jump.

"Mr Devereux, please come with me to my office at once," she said in her no-nonsense voice.

Guy followed her, relieved to have a bit of a break from washing plates. When they reached Miss Liddington's office, Angel was waiting outside. She looked at Guy in confusion and they both shrugged their shoulders.

"Come in and take a seat please," instructed Miss Liddington, indicating the same two chairs that Guy and Angel sat in previously.

"I'm afraid you haven't passed your week's trial," began Miss Liddington to Guy and Angel's astonishment. "Unfortunately, Miss Jasmine we have found some literature in your room that gives us cause for concern."

"Literature?" questioned Angel rather confused.

"Indeed, a suffragette newspaper and a handwritten address of a meeting time and place," replied Miss Liddington, staring intently at Angel.

"You have been in my bag, that's private," said Angel, looking from Miss Liddington to Guy.

"We need to know everything we can about our employees, what choice do we have? And we have been justified in our actions. As a suffragette young lady, you are a risk to the hotel's good reputation. Goodness only knows what you are planning to disrupt here. It makes me shudder to think the King and Queen came here to dinner with the Prime Minister, as they do often. Were you planning to empty a dinner plate on the King's head? Pour wine on the Queen?"

"Of course not, I'm not actually a suffragette, I just bumped into some, they gave me the magazine and invited me to a meeting. I haven't been and I would have been working anyway as it was held during the day," said Angel defending herself.

"Well, I cannot take a chance, if you cause any disruption here, I will lose my job," said Miss Liddington. "A couple of years ago two suffragettes disguised themselves as orange sellers in Liverpool. In actual fact they had catapults and they attacked Prime Minister Asquith's car."

"It's fine Miss Liddington," said Guy. "We understand. I can assure you Angel would never cause any disruption here, but we know you can't take that chance."

"Thank you, Mr Devereux. Even if Angel chose not to humiliate us, she is in contact with suffragettes and that draws their attention to the Hotel Victoria."

"I understand," said Angel. "Are we to leave now?"

"Yes, here are your wages." Miss Liddington handed them a small brown envelope each. "I am afraid I cannot give you a reference either, the Hotel Victoria cannot be seen to be recommending a suffragette. You must go back to your rooms and gather your belongings now. You were both very hard workers; I shall be sorry to see you go."

Once back in the corridor Guy and Angel looked at each other in disbelief.

"Fired for associating with a suffragette, that's brilliant," laughed Guy as they walked up the staff stairs to their rooms. "Don't worry Angel, we were leaving tomorrow anyway, our quest for the missing egg is the overall picture, you said so yourself." Guy rubbed Angel's arm; he was concerned as she was very quiet.

"You're right, I know, I'm just a bit shocked

to be fired," said Angel.

"Well at least your livelihood doesn't depend on it, just as well as we didn't get references. We achieved what we came here to do, locate Ottomar and Beatrice."

"Again, you're right Guy, let's just move on. Shall we find Ottomar and say goodbye?"

"Definitely, although he will be busy with serving breakfast at the moment, but we can give him a quick handshake. He seems like a nice man, such a shame…" Guy stopped what he was about to say. "We also need to say goodbye to Ted, he has been very helpful."

*

They collected their belongings, which in Guy's case was just his clothes, so he changed back into them. They found Ted on reception and said goodbye. Ted seemed sorry to see them go but agreed with Miss Liddington, the Hotel Victoria's reputation came first. They then went to the restaurant and peered in hoping to see Ottomar.

"You really will need to leave now," said the familiar sharp tones of Miss Liddington. "Out through the staff entrance at the back please."

Reluctantly Guy and Angel made their way out through the back entrance, to the little staff courtyard area, to their surprise Ottomar was standing there, with his head in his hands.

"Ottomar, Mr Waibel," called Guy. "Is everything well with you?"

"Oh, hello," said Ottomar, his voice cracking as he spoke.

"Whatever is wrong?" asked Angel.

"It's so sad, but after you left my family yesterday, a little while later some more visitors came, but they were not so friendly. Two men nearly bashed our door down, my children had to hide under the bed, terrified for their lives."

Guy and Angel looked at each other in horror and then back to Ottomar, they knew what he was about to tell them.

"My wife was gifted a very expensive present when she left her job to marry me. The old lady she worked for loved Beatrice and she gave her a Faberge egg. It was probably worth a lot of money, but Beatrice decided to just hide it away for the future, which is so uncertain." Ottomar raised his hands and shrugged his shoulders. "You know, what with war looming, I may be sent away, back to Germany."

Guy and Angel exchanged a glance, Guy noticed tears welling in Angel's eyes at Ottomar's last remark. She composed herself quickly.

"These two men forced my wife to hand over the egg and not only that they forced her to sign the ownership papers over to Henry

Towers, the old lady's nephew. He couldn't bear that Beatrice had been gifted the egg, he had her arrested over it a few months ago. His business is in danger of closing, and he feels threatened by German competition. I expect that's why he can't bear Beatrice having the egg." Ottomar shook his head and looked at the ground. "What an awful man to subject Beatrice and the children to that ordeal."

"Ottomar, that is terrible, I'm so sorry to hear about it," said Angel. "Will your wife go to the police?"

"She said not, Beatrice thinks that he will never give up and she doesn't want to put the children's lives at risk again. She said it is best gone," said Ottomar sadly. "They could have hurt my family yesterday and I think she is right. The Faberge egg has only brought trouble, especially in the last year, it is definitely best gone."

"That is an awful story," said Guy. "There are some very mean and wicked people around, they will get their comeuppance one day, I'm sure of it. Your family are lovely and didn't deserve to be treated in that way."

"Thank you for your kind words. Where are you going? Are you leaving?" asked Ottomar.

"We got fired," said Angel. "Miss Liddington thinks I'm a suffragette, I'm not but I understand her concerns."

"I'm sorry to hear that, you are both so kind. What will you do now?"

"We will move on to another town and find work, it's no problem," said Angel smiling, reassuring Ottomar they were both fine.

"It has been a pleasure to meet you both," said Ottomar shaking their hands.

"You too," said Guy. "Your family are safe, just enjoy your days out together. Money doesn't buy happiness."

Ottomar smiled. "Wise words young man, wise words."

"It was a pleasure to meet your family too," said Angel. "I'm just so sorry we didn't stay longer yesterday, maybe we could have helped."

"I think it is a good job you were not there. My family will be fine, please do not worry about us, we move on." Ottomar smiled, straightened his apron. "Goodbye and take care, I hope you find work soon." With that message he went back through the door to resume serving breakfast.

"Claude got the day wrong," said Angel shaking her head. "Why did we rely on the memory of a five-year-old?"

"He was only two days out, to be fair," said Guy. "But they are two crucial days for us."

"On to Manchester then I guess," said Angel. "We need to find Henry Towers' factory and track him down. The egg will doubtless be in Manchester by now."

Guy nodded in agreement, they left the hotel through the back entrance and walked to Trafalgar Square one last time.

*

At Marylebone station the noise of the steam trains puffing and whistling was overwhelming, making it hard for Guy and Angel to hold a conversation.

"So, we are looking for the Great Central Railway line to Manchester – London Road station," shouted Guy. "Never heard of it, it must be an old one not used anymore."

"It's going to be a long day. Shall we get a magazine to read on the journey?" said Angel, scarcely audible but pointing to a kiosk.

At the kiosk Angel picked up a black and white magazine called *The Sketch,* which had a photo of a very abstract statue on the front. Guy went for a copy of *The Strand* magazine, printed in blue and white on the front, it promised to tell him all about the story Captain Scott. Angel paid for the magazines and they went off in search of their train to Manchester.

*

Guy put his magazine down and yawned. "This is making me sleepy," he said looking out of the window. "You know what Angel, I've been thinking, I reckon those two men that barged into us at the Oval station were the thieves."

"That's a bit of an assumption, but actually it wouldn't surprise me, they weren't nice men, were they?" Angel put her magazine down on the seat, she was facing Guy and they were the only two in their compartment.

"What are we going to do when we get to Manchester?" asked Guy. "How can we track down Henry Towers? Even if we find his factory, he might not be there."

"I know and I've thought of something else that Ottomar said." Angel sighed, looking out of the window at the fields beyond and then back to Guy. "Even if we track the stolen egg and bring it back to the twenty-first century, Barbara will not be able to prove it belongs to her family without those ownership papers being in her name."

"I hadn't thought of that," said Guy. "What on earth are we going to do? Henry Towers will never sign the egg over to Beatrice."

"We need to find out something about him, that's what we need," said Angel.

"Are you talking about blackmail? Angel!" said Guy wide eyed.

"Afraid so. Look Guy, this man is in financial difficulties, so much so he is prepared to commit a crime by stealing the Faberge egg from Beatrice and whilst that is worth a lot of money, I'm a hundred percent sure that it won't be enough to save his factory."

"I see where you're going," nodded Guy.

"He must be involved in other criminal activity; we just need to find out what it is and present him with our evidence."

"But Angel, he knows some quite nasty people." Guy's eyes became wide and he looked worried.

"We need to corner him, on his own, in his house, because that is where the egg is probably hidden and remember the egg never comes to light again," said Angel, with the beginning of a plan formulating.

"You are quite fearless, aren't you? The Captain Scott of treasure recovery," said Guy pointing to his magazine. "Or *Indiana Jones* as we would call you in my day."

"She sounds interesting. I'd like to meet her."

"He's a man and he is fictional, there are a series of films about him. He doesn't like snakes."

"Oh, well let's hope the only snake we meet is Henry Towers," said Angel laughing but with sense of trepidation. "How can we get to meet him? We need to have a think."

The couple sat in silence for a while, only speaking to the train conductor when he came through to check their tickets. They rested their heads on the back of the seats deep in thought.

Suddenly Guy leapt forward, "Mrs Pankhurst," he shouted excitedly. "She is in Manchester."

At this moment the train went into a tunnel and any thought of being able to speak was put on hold because of the noise and the dark. The tunnel seemed to go on forever, as Guy was poised to continue his speech. Finally, the train emerged into daylight and normal conversation could resume.

"Would we be able to find her?" said Angel hopefully.

"Angel, not only does she have a big reception at Manchester Town Hall this weekend, I know where she lives," said Guy triumphantly.

"You do? How?"

"My mum, you know I told you she loves history. Well one time when my dad took me see Manchester United, mum and Mark came along too. We stayed in Manchester all weekend and after the match mum took us to various places: the library, a park, the art gallery and a famous writer's house, but she also took us to the Pankhurst Centre."

"And their address was displayed there?" asked Angel confused.

"No Angel, better than that, the Pankhurst Centre is in their old house." Guy sat back looking very pleased with himself.

"No way!" said Angel. "Would you be able to find it?"

"Yes, I think so, it was in the east of Manchester just below where Man City play at the Etihad Stadium. It was by a hospital, but that might not be there yet. Anyway, I'd know when I see it."

"Well, that's our job for tomorrow then, track down Mrs Pankhurst, she will know Henry Towers, or at least know someone who knows him. It's a start and it's better than nothing."

*

Guy and Angel tried to resume reading their magazines, but they were too excited to concentrate properly. Angel stared at Guy, looking as though she was going to ask him a question, but she wasn't yet sure of the question she wanted to ask.

"What?" said Guy. "Is something wrong?"

"No, nothing's wrong, I was just wondering about your family history, before Guy the First."

"Random thought, why are you wondering about that?"

"I just wondered how Guy the First had enough money to build that lovely big house where the treasure was buried."

"Devereux Hall, yeah it is epic isn't it. Gramps always says it would be cold in the winter though and it's just as well we don't live there anymore." Guy looked out at the sheep grazing in a field, then turned back. "Guy the First didn't build it actually, his father did, Guy was the first child, and the oldest son, born in the new house. Guy's dad wanted to start a new era for the family."

"Oh, I see, how did they make their money though?"

"Farming, rent from the properties they owned in the local area, you know, like Morely's farm where we stayed. I'm sure they invested money in new ventures, trade for example."

"The transatlantic slave trade?"

Guy looked down, his lips tight together before facing Angel again. "I am so sorry, but yes, it was in its early stages back then, but we do believe they were part of it."

Guy and Angel were quiet for a few minutes, lost in their own thoughts.

"It happened Guy and we can't change that, but I do think that subsequent generations should acknowledge it and, in some way, make up for it. Even if not financially, then raising awareness of what happened to the millions of Africans stolen from their lands and forced into brutal slave labour conditions, and they were brutal."

"You've visited, haven't you?"

"Yeah, I have." Angel looked out of the window and wiped away her tears. "Another time, I will tell you about it another time. I promise. But what I was wondering is where the Devereux name came from, it's not English?"

"That I do know, it's French, Norman actually, it was originally de Devereux and can be traced back to the Battle of Hastings in 1066."

"Oh, so your family came over as part of the Norman Conquest then?"

"That's right, there were four brothers, they all fought at Hastings, so did their father, he died on the battlefield. The four brothers, like many other Norman knights, were sent to different parts of England to establish a base and squash local rebellions. Alain de Devereux was sent to Essex and he is our ancestor."

"Wow, so good to know your family history, did your grandad research it?"

"He did, although a lot of it has been passed down through the generations, and the Internet makes it easy these days."

Guy wanted to ask Angel about her family history, he didn't really know if Angel's had a family history at all, but he felt it was not the right time to ask, and Angel had now resumed reading her magazine. That conversation would have to wait for another day.

*

When they got off the train at London Road station, Guy stood on the platform in amazement. Before him were the familiar green and white columns, leading to the ironwork roof of Manchester Piccadilly, a station he knew well. Tears filled his eyes as remembered being at the station with his dad, enroute to Old Trafford to see United play.

"Hey, you ok?" asked Angel, seeing his emotional response to the station. "Oh, you came here with your dad, didn't you."

"Happy memories Angel, but sad too as I don't get to come here with my dad anymore." Guy gave another glance around at the familiar buildings. "Come on let's not hang around, it's been a long day, which started with us getting fired."

Outside the station it was dusk, but Guy was in for another shock. He stood looking around in amazement, unable to speak for a moment.

"Guy, what is it?" asked Angel.

"Manchester..." said Guy. "It's so different. I mean I know it's a northern industrial town, but wow, there are so many chimneys and so much smoke. It doesn't look like the same place."

"I guess that's the thing about time travel, places looked and felt different in the past," said Angel.

"And smelt different too, the smoke in the air is over whelming," Guy coughed as if to make his point.

"Well let's hope we find this egg soon then," said Angel, pulling Guy in the direction of the town.

After checking in to a little hotel near the station, Guy and Angel had some dinner in the restaurant then said goodnight as they went into their respective rooms. Guy tried to get some sleep before their big day tracking down Mrs Pankhurst, in order to track down Henry Towers, but in truth he had a very disturbed night's sleep, wondering how on earth they were going to get this awful man to sign the Faberge egg back over to Beatrice Waibel.

Chapter 11 – Friday 31st October 1913

"Look at that suffragette poster, *The Cat and Mouse Act,* that's very dramatic," said Angel pointing to a row of posters on a wall near their hotel. "The huge golden cat, with what looks like a dead suffragette in its mouth. Crikey, it makes the point doesn't it."

Guy sighed. "I remember analysing that poster in History once, never thought I'd be helping a suffragette escape the clutches of the cat."

"Well, it is a good job we did, it gives us a link to Henry Towers," said Angel looking at the poster.

"I still can't get over the amount of chimneys here," said Guy pointing to the skyline. "Now it's daylight we have the whole picture. I just didn't realise there were quite so many factories here at this time. No wonder all the redbrick is so dirty."

"It's certainly a very industrial landscape, chimneys and factories in all directions. Where do we begin Guy? You lead the way."

"Ok, well we are pretty central at the moment, we need to go southeast."

"Should we just head for Manchester City's ground and go south?" asked Angel.

"I actually have no idea where City played in 1913," laughed Guy, "my Manchester football history is all United. Anyway, let's just head in this direction, it feels right."

They set off, crossing the road and dodging the traffic, which was just as busy as London.

"What are we going to say to Mrs Pankhurst?" asked Guy. "We can't tell her about the robbery, she will tell us to go to the police."

"We could say he took something belonging to a friend of ours and she would like it back. We could say it was a misunderstanding and she has sent us to try and sort it out," said Angel thoughtfully.

"Yeah, ok, it's all we've got," said Guy nodding his head.

*

"I recognise this building," said Guy pointing to the Plymouth Grove pub as they walked past. "It's got a clock tower, yes look, see there at the side."

"It's very distinctive," said Angel looking at the huge redbrick pub, with a central door flanked by two columns on each side.

"I think it's Chinese restaurant now. Oh, I do miss takeaways actually," said Guy with a sudden longing for more typical twenty-first century food.

"Well, more importantly, are we any closer to the Pankhurst's house?" asked Angel.

"Yes, I think we are, the writer's house we visited is further down this road, the Pankhurst's house is about five minutes' walk from here. We need to go back and turn off to the left."

Guy led the way and Angel turned to follow.

"Who was the writer that lived in the house down this road?" asked Angel.

"Oh, I can't remember to be honest, a Victorian woman. Mum was all misty-eyed walking round the house, you know how mum's can be. Actually, do you know how mum's can be? Sorry I just assumed …"

"I do indeed know how mum's can be." Angel laughed at Guy's awkwardness.

"You just don't say much about your life."

"I'm not really allowed to, that's the rules. Is this where we turn?"

After walking for another few minutes following the turning, Guy started to look around in earnest.

"It's round here to the left somewhere." Guy followed a little road and stopped outside a redbrick building surrounded by black railings. A short path led to a front door, a window either side, one of which was bay fronted. On the first floor there were three smaller windows.

"This is definitely it, one hundred percent," said Guy confidently.

"Might as well knock then," said Angel with some trepidation.

"Mrs Pankhurst will think we are mad, or stalkers?" said Guy looking worried.

"No time like the present, let's get on with it." Angel walked up the path and knocked on the door.

*

The room was impressive with three big arched windows, although upon further inspection, Guy saw that the middle window was in fact French doors out to a little patio area. The wallpaper was light and flowery for the top two thirds and green on the bottom third. A little piano was pushed against a wall. On the opposite wall there was a fireplace, with a mirror above and further round there was a large dresser, stacked with blue and white china plates. A small staircase led out of the room. Guy looked across the table he was seated at, in awe of the woman opposite, a woman he was rather shocked to be meeting for the second time.

"Henry Towers is thoroughly unpleasant," said Mrs Pankhurst, taking a sip of her tea. "Haven't I always said that Adela," she addressed her youngest daughter. "He doesn't support the cause and tries to prevent his wife from meeting with us. To her credit though Mrs Towers does get here when she can, and she was involved in getting support for our cause among her social circle. I really don't know how she puts up with him."

"He only married her for her parents' money," said Adela.

"Very true," said Mrs Pankhurst. "So, he has something that belongs to friend of yours, you say? A mix up? Likely story, I imagine he stole it."

"He has no morals," added Adela. "He is, however, due to be at our reception on Sunday afternoon at the Town Hall."

"Yes, he will be, won't he, that's true," said Mrs Pankhurst thoughtfully. "Oh, he isn't there to support votes for women. He will be there to make connections for himself."

"Mrs Towers wanted him to come, she hoped if talked to other men who support our cause, it might change his mind," said Adela pouring more tea and helping herself to a biscuit. She then offered the biscuit plate round to Guy and

Angel.

"Come along to the reception," said Mrs Pankhurst, "listen to his conversations see what you can find out. If nothing else you will get to meet him, build up a picture of him, it might help."

Guy and Angel nodded in agreement to Mrs Pankhurst's plan.

"Meanwhile Miss Jasmine, we have a very important meeting here tomorrow night and I need young energetic women like yourself to help and support a project I am working on. It will highlight the issue of votes for women and make us front page news. Will you come? It starts at seven pm."

Angel looked at Guy, who was wide eyed.

"Yes of course, I'd love to join you, it will be an honour," said Angel, looking away from Guy and smiling at Mrs Pankhurst.

*

"Angel, what are you thinking?" said Guy as they walked back towards the city centre.

"She has been very kind, we have to give something back, I couldn't really say no."

"I suppose, but you can't get involved in their activities, otherwise you will be in prison and then what will I do?"

"Don't panic, I'm only going to the

Pankhurst's house, that's it, I promise."

Guy smiled. "If you promise. Shame I didn't have this experience before I sat my History GCSE, my grade would have been a lot higher."

Chapter 12 – Saturday 1st November 1913

"Shall we have a walk around the city centre?" said Angel. "We have got all day to explore Manchester and it looks quite sunny out, not what I was expecting."

"Mad fer it, yeah!" Guy did a Liam Gallagher style swagger as he walked out of the hotel.

Angel rolled her eyes and they both laughed as they linked arms to go and explore.

The couple enjoyed themselves looking in shop windows under the canopies. Manchester was a bustling city, with people going about their Saturday business. In the distance chimneys were still puffing away, despite it being the weekend. Guy and Angel marvelled at the grand Victorian buildings, pointing out places of interest to each other. Eventually they came across the huge arched building of another station, Manchester Central Railway.

"I recognise this building, but I don't think it

is a station now," said Guy as they both looked at the vast glass arch on their way in to look around.

"Impressive building, it's like a huge glass cavern, the Victorians did like these ironwork and glass structures didn't they," said Angel, turning round to look at Guy.

Guy, however, was fixated on one of the noticeboards, reading intently as if his life depended on it.

"Angel, it's Saturday," said Guy eventually.

"That's right, Guy, Saturday 1st November."

"You know what traditionally happened on Saturdays at three o'clock don't you?"

"Not really," replied Angel.

"Kick off, Angel, kick off happened." Guy was still facing the noticeboard.

Angel followed Guy's gaze and read the sign out loud. "Match day special shuttle service to United Football Ground, Manchester United v Liverpool, three o'clock kick off."

Guy turned to look at Angel, with what could only be described as pleading eyes. "Can we? Can we go? Oh my God, can we go and see United play Liverpool?"

"Do we have a choice?" said Angel, shaking her head, but smiling all the same. "I've never been to a football match. Is it at Old Trafford?"

"Yeah, it is, they moved there in 1910, but it's not called Old Trafford yet, that comes later. This is beyond exciting, forget meeting kings and famous historical figures, I'm going to see Manchester United play Liverpool in 1913. I wonder who wins?"

"Well, by five o'clock you'll know," said Angel, helpfully.

"I will, won't I, oh thank you so much for this. Let's go and get a train ticket, come on."

Half an hour later, Guy and Angel were sitting on the Match Day Special steam train, chugging their way out to the Trafford area of Manchester. On the train with them were hundreds of excited Manchester United fans, chatting away about the prospect of beating Liverpool. The fans were mostly men, wearing suits and waistcoats and peaked caps, very much the same clothes that Guy was wearing. There were also a few women, in their long dark coats, wearing hats which were quite elaborately decorated with flowers.

"I hope I'm not sitting behind one of those big hats," said Angel. "I won't be able to see a thing."

Guy laughed. "You won't be sitting at all actually. It will be standing only, is that ok?"

"Right, I didn't realise, yes, it will be fine," replied Angel.

"I don't know when seats were first introduced at Old Trafford, but after the Hillsborough Disaster in 1989, it became an all-seater stadium."

"What was the Hillsborough Disaster?" asked Angel.

"It was an FA Cup semi-final at Sheffield United's ground, too many people crowded onto the terraces at one end. It led to a huge crush and ninety-two Liverpool fans died."

"That's awful, how terrifying for everyone involved. I cannot imagine the crush."

"Yeah, it's still in the news now. So that's why everyone has to have a seat back in the present. Don't worry though, nothing will happen today, because if there had been disaster, I'd know about it. I've watched enough documentaries about the history of the club."

"That's a relief then, but you don't know the score today."

"No, but I don't think this was a great season for us. We'd won the league in about 1908, we won the FA Cup the next season, Billy Meredith was the star player in those days, but then around the time of the war, maybe just after, we got relegated."

"You have spent a lot of time on the history of Manchester United, I'm impressed."

"Oh, Angel, I've just thought, Billy Meredith might be playing today, this is insane."

"Will you recognise him?"

"Absolutely, I had a picture of him on my bedroom wall for years."

"You did! That is dedication to the club Guy."

"Well, it was a poster of United stars past and present. I realise I sound a bit of a United nerd, but that's the way it is. Anyway, he is tall, short dark hair and a large bushy moustache."

"That describes half of this crowd," said Angel looking around laughing.

When they got to their stop everyone piled off the train and Guy and Angel went along with the flow of the crowd. It wasn't long before they were standing outside the stadium that Guy was very familiar with.

"The Theatre of Dreams, not quite as big as it is now, and no Mega Store or Hotel Football." Guy was quite misty eyed.

"Hey, are you ok?" Angel put her arm around Guy's shoulder. "After all we have been through, I don't think I have ever seen you this emotional."

"I'm just feeling honoured really. Am I dreaming?"

"No, you're not. Come on let's go in." Angel linked her arm with Guy's and steered him off to the turnstiles. "Where do you want to go in?"

"Stretford End, I'm not sure if it is called that yet, but it's a no brainer."

*

Standing on a very different Stretford End, Guy looked down at the programme he had purchased for a penny outside the stadium and then joined in with the cheering as Manchester United ran on to the pitch, wearing their traditional red, Liverpool were in an all-white away kit.

"There he is Angel, that's Billy Meredith, unbelievable, just wow!" Guy stared in awe at the mythical player who had adorned his bedroom wall. "Also, wow, look at that referee suit, how on earth is he going to run about in a suit for ninety minutes?"

"It doesn't look very comfortable does it, mind you look at the players' boots, they look so heavy."

"Don't they, glad things have moved on, I wouldn't fancy ninety minutes in that kit."

The referee blew the whistle and the match was underway. It wasn't long before Manchester United were running with the ball to the opposite end from Guy and Angel, much to the excitement of the crowd around them. The ball was passed to the number eleven, who calmly took his moment and shot straight into the back of the net. The crowd jumped and cheered.

A name was being chanted by some of the crowd, "Wall, Wall, Wall."

"Wow, three minutes, that's amazing," said Angel. "Great start."

"Isn't it, you wouldn't believe the times my dad brought me all the way up to Manchester when I was little and it would be a nil, nil draw. You are honoured Angel," Guy gave her hug and continued with his cheering.

"Oh no, here come Liverpool," said Guy, as three Liverpool players broke away and hurtled towards them. The player on the ball reached the penalty box and a United player tackled him, the ball was saved but the Liverpool player went down. There were shouts of a penalty from the Liverpool fans, but the referee was undeterred and play continued. "No VAR to check that one," laughed Guy, happy the penalty had not been given.

"VAR?" quizzed Angel.

"Video assistant referee," replied Guy.

"Oh, no, not yet."

"Not for over hundred years yet," confirmed Guy.

Liverpool were on the attack again, but

United intercepted a pass and charged off down the other end, it came to nothing but the crowd cheered and clapped in appreciation of the move anyway.

The half time whistle blew and the score was still one, nil to Manchester United. Guy took the time to read through the little programme, it was mostly adverts for local tailors and furniture shops, but the team line up was presented, along with a message from the manager, Tom Watson.

"I'm quite peckish," said Angel, shivering in the cold November air.

"I doubt they are selling United's famous pies just yet; you might have to wait until after the game," said Guy, "Is that ok?"

"Of course, let's get some fish and chips after the match," said Angel, rubbing her gloved hands together and then putting them in her pockets. She moved closer to Guy to shelter from the wind and Guy smiled as she did so.

It wasn't long before both teams were back out on the pitch and Billy Meredith was charging down the right wing towards them, as he did so Guy felt the crowd surge towards the pitch. Meredith crossed the ball and Wall couldn't quite connect, so the ball went behind for a goal kick, to a collective sigh from the United supporters.

The game was quite tight, both teams attacking, the attacks not ending in a goal and the action moving towards the other end. Then in the eighty eighth minute, Billy Meredith made another cross into United's number ten, he met the cross with his head. The ball landed straight in the back of the net and the crowd roared to celebrate, the name West being chanted this time.

Liverpool kicked off, but the ball was intercepted by Wall, and he just kept going, weaving this way and that, head down, but knowing exactly what he wanted to do. From just outside the box, he finally took his shot, it went straight over the keeper's head and into the top left corner of the net. The second goal in two minutes sent the crowd wild. Liverpool kicked off again but had made little progress before the final whistle blew, confirming Manchester United had won by three goals to nil. Guy cheered and just about stopped himself from singing a twenty-first century chant, not that anyone would have heard him with the noise the crowd were making.

"Shall we get back to the centre and then have fish and chips?" said Angel. "We don't want to miss the match day special train."

"Good idea, it might be a bit of a wait though," replied Guy, tucking his programme into his pocket. "We don't want you late for your suffragette meeting, do we?"

Angel shook her head. "No, we don't, but we have plenty of time before seven o'clock.

*

"What do you reckon? As good as Southend?" Angel was tucking in to her second ever fish and chips, she added some more vinegar to the chips she had missed.

"About the same I'd say. I'm surprised there's no gravy though, they do love gravy on their fish and chips in Manchester, it must be a more recent addition," said Guy lining up a particularly fluffy white piece of cod.

"Did you say gravy?" Angel pulled a face.

"It's quite nice to be honest, it feels weird eating fish and chips in Manchester without it," Guy laughed as Angel shook her head.

"Seriously though Angel, I'm worried about you meeting with the suffragettes, they do crazy stunts, if you end up getting arrested and sent to prison, how will I survive? How will I get the egg back?" Guy was clearly stressed; it had been playing on his mind all day. "Look if you want to fight for votes for women, let's look up one of the suffragist groups, there are loads in Manchester. You can hand out leaflets or something, anything that you won't be arrested for."

"Relax Guy, whilst I do of course want women to have a vote, that's not the reason I'm going to the meeting. We know women get the vote. No, the reason I'm going, is that Mrs Pankhurst is well-connected in Manchester, Mrs

Towers comes to the meetings, they are useful for our cause, returning the Faberge egg to Barbara. I'm not going to get involved in stunts and arson campaigns," said Angel trying to reassure Guy. "Now let's eat this before it goes cold.

Guy nodded, but he was not convinced.

*

"Here we are then," said Guy standing in front of the Pankhurst's house. "I'm going to wait for you in the Plymouth Grove pub."

"Good idea, I will come and meet you when the meeting is over, it's just one meeting Guy, it will be interesting and useful."

Angel turned from Guy and walked up the path, as she did so a suffragette opened the front door.

"Angel Jasmine, so good to see you," said Sarah giving her a hug. "What are you doing in Manchester?"

"Trying to find something for a friend," replied Angel. "I guess you are hiding from the police back in London."

"I certainly am," said Sarah. "Come in, come in."

The door shut behind them and Guy was left under the lamplight on a cold Manchester street, he walked round to the Plymouth Grove pub, keen to get in the warm. The pub was busy, mostly men sitting on benches, their beer resting on the tables, as they chatted away about the matters of the day. A piano was being played and a few of the men were singing along with some of the women. It was quite smoky, which made Guy cough as he walked across the sawdust-covered floor to the bar.

"Young man, what canna I get you?" asked the barman, a tea towel slung casually over his shoulder, as he wiped his hands on his grubby white apron.

Noticing bottles of lemonade behind the bar Guy thought that would be the best choice, so he asked for one. As the barman poured the lemonade into a glass, Guy was sure he could see a marble in the neck of the chunky glass bottle. The barman put the bottle into a crate, Guy presumed this would be washed and reused, and he handed the drink over. Guy paid, still craning his neck to look at the bottle, whilst the barman looked at him in confusion and shook his head.

Noticing a small empty table at the side of the pub, under a poster advertising an exhibition of Egyptian artefacts at the Manchester Museum, Guy positioned himself so that he could see the door and Angel when she arrived. He took off his cap, put it on the table and got his Manchester United programme out of his pocket. He tried to take his mind off the suffragette meeting by reading it, but the thought of what Angel might get roped into was distracting him.

Looking around the pub, Guy realised that a group of men sitting in a huddle just behind him were very familiar. They were wearing suits not red shirts, but Billy Meredith was unmistakable, Guy could not believe his eyes for a second or two, he then realised he was staring and looked away quickly.

Pushing his chair back a little, Guy shifted his position to see if he could overhear their conversation, pretending all the while, that he was very focused on the front door and looking out for someone. He managed to hear some of the conversation, just the odd word, Billy Meredith's Welsh accent standing out from the other voices. Guy thought the conversation was to do with players' rights, but he couldn't be sure, although he was sure that Billy Meredith was the only one of the group drinking lemonade.

Glancing through the football programme once more, but with an ear still to the group behind him, Guy jumped out of his skin as a loud Welsh voice addressed him.

"Would you like me to sign that lad?"

Guy looked up to see Billy Meredith's piercing blue eyes staring back down at him.

"Sorry lad, I didn't mean to scare you," Billy laughed and Guy relaxed a little.

"Ye, yes - if, if - you could, th - that really would be amazing, thank you." Guy was embarrassed that he wasn't acting cool, he hadn't stuttered that much when David Beckham signed a copy of a programme for him at a charity event.

Billy produced a very stylish ink pen from his jacket pocket and signed the front of the programme.

"Did you enjoy the match today then?" asked Billy.

"Very much, always good to beat Liverpool," said Guy regaining the power of speech.

"You from down south then?"

"Yes, near London, but I'm big United fan, always have been."

"Must be difficult to follow us down there," said Billy.

"Not as hard as you would think," said Guy, smiling and wondering what Billy would make of twenty-first century football. "I get up here when I can."

"Lucky lad, well you take care now and safe journey back down south." With that Billy strode across the pub to the front door and disappeared into the night, Guy staring in awe after him.

Guy traced Billy's signature on the programme, shaking his head, he wondered if he could ever get used to time travel, or would it continue to blow his mind? Then another thought came to him, would it continue at all? He couldn't think about that, not now.

He turned to look at the group of players behind him, still engrossed in their conversation, they were a lot younger than Billy. Some of them would volunteer to go to France and fight in the trenches and some of them would later be called up to fight. Looking round the pub, Guy realised he was looking at future *pals battalions*, where groups of young men joined up together to fight in the war, not knowing the horror ahead and that many of them would die together.

At that moment the door opened and Angel walked in, she beckoned Guy to her, he jumped up grabbing his cap and now precious programme, and made his way over to her.

"Angel, am I please to see you." Guy put an arm around her shoulder.

"Are you ok? You look a bit shaken, what's happened?" said Angel concerned for her travellee.

"I just felt as though I wanted to shout at all those young men, don't go to France, don't sign up, don't be *pals battalions*, and I know I can't, and I didn't, but I feel responsible because some of them, too many of them, will die. These pubs will be empty soon, the men's football league will be suspended, the women will take over, life will never be the same again for this generation and if that's not enough, if they survive, they have the Blitz in World War Two to follow. It just feels hopeless." Guy was breathless at the end of his monologue.

Angel hugged him. "I'm sorry, this is difficult, I don't think I really took on board how difficult this can be. All I can say is, we can't change history, but in certain circumstances, we can make the future a bit more pleasant for some people. It's only a little joy, compared to the misery of the past but it's all we can do and so we will do it, together."

Guy sighed. "I'm sorry, I got overwhelmed for a minute in there."

"Hey Guy, it's understandable," said Angel as they linked arms and began the walk back to the hotel.

Angel was very quiet and she too looked as though she had a lot on her mind.

"How was Sarah? She has obviously escaped being re-arrested," Guy's breath was visible in the cold night air as he spoke.

"She was fine, in good spirits actually," said Angel smiling.

"Was Letitia Towers there?"

"No, she had sent her apologies, it's Saturday night, I'm sure she had a function to attend or something." Angel was still distracted by her thoughts.

"Ok Angel, something is wrong, you are really quiet." Guy stopped and stood in front of

Angel blocking her path.

Angel looked up at Guy. "You were right about their tactics; they want to keep the issue of votes for women in the public eye."

"What have you agreed to do?"

"Nothing, nothing at all Guy, honestly, only to attend meetings, that's it." Angel took Guy's hands in hers. "Honestly I am not going to get involved in any stunt."

"What are they planning then?"

"Guy, you can't alert anyone, you know that don't you. We are not from this time, we have job to do, which we are allowed to do because it won't change anything. Everything else must happen."

"You are worrying me now Angel."

"They are planning to bomb the cactus house in Alexandra Park," said Angel.

"What on earth? Seriously?"

"During the night obviously, no one will be hurt," clarified Angel.

"Even so. What are they bombing it with? I mean how do they get bombs?"

"They are making it with a pipe."

"And they think this will convince a parliament full of men to give them the vote?"

"It's complicated isn't it," said Angel. "Their

hearts are in the right place."

The couple resumed walking the mile route back to the hotel.

"When they bomb Alexandra Park, bombs will go off at Kew Gardens in London and another park near Bristol," added Angel.

"Wow, that is some co-ordination. Anything else?" asked Guy.

"A continued focus on breaking windows of significant buildings."

"I'm surprised they are letting Mrs Pankhurst use Manchester Town Hall tomorrow," said Guy.

"They don't actually realise it is a suffragette meeting, they think it is a local council meeting. Some local councillors who support the cause have booked the room."

"I see, I hope it doesn't turn violent tomorrow." Guy shook his head.

"Mrs Pankhurst was so engaging though, she ended by saying *I incite this meeting to rebellion*."

"Well, we just need to start our detective work on Henry Towers tomorrow," said Guy. "The sooner we get out of here the better."

"Amen to that," said Angel, looking up at the moon.

Chapter 13 – Sunday 2nd November 1913

"I've been thinking," said Angel over breakfast in the hotel. "I think we should draw up a letter for Henry Towers to sign, one that confirms Beatrice Waibel as the rightful owner of the egg."

"Yes, let's do that, good idea," said Guy as he finished his egg and bacon. "God knows how we will get him to sign it though."

"Something will turn up, we just have to keep our ears and eyes open," said Angel with more confidence than her eyes betrayed.

*

"Here it is look," Guy handed Angel a piece of paper. "They have thought of everything, paper, pen and an inkwell, all on the desk in our little rooms."

"Ok, let's think about this." Angel sat down at the desk and picked up the ink pen, holding it poised to write.

After some discussion the pair had

composed a statement that ensured it was clear Beatrice owned the Faberge egg.

I, Mr Henry Towers, do hereby declare that the Faberge egg, previously given to Mrs Beatrice Waibel, wife of Mr Ottomar Waibel, both of 149 Coronation Buildings, by my aunt, Mrs Elizabeth Towers, widow of Mr Charles Towers, both from Westminster, does belong to Mrs Beatrice Waibel. She is the rightful and undisputed owner of the Faberge egg.

Signed   *Date*

"Brilliant, now we just have to find him and ask him to sign it," said Guy sighing.

"I have a present for you Guy." Angel picked up a pile of clothes that were neatly folded on her bed.

"I did wonder what they were," said Guy, taking the clothes from Angel.

"A smart black and white pin stripe suit and waistcoat, crisp white shirt, dark grey tie and a little bowler hat. I thought that we needed smartening up a bit for the reception at Manchester Town Hall, so that we blend in with the business crowd a bit more."

"Thank you, great idea. Where did you get them from?"

"My bag of course," said Angel with a wink.

"More crypticness." Guy rolled his eyes and ran a hand over the pin stripe suit. "What have you got?"

"Green velvet ankle length skirt and matching jacket," said Angel picking up her suit. "A black coat coming down to my calves, well I was cold last night, and a black hat with green velvet trim, not too big eh." Angel posed in her hat.

"Nice hat, it suits you. And you're right, we do need to look the part a bit more. I'd best get changed then."

*

"It really is an amazing Victorian building," Guy was looking up at the elaborate and gothic Manchester Town Hall. The central clock tower rose majestically to a pointed spire above the main entrance, which was an arched doorway.

Several suffragettes were guiding people into the banqueting room, Guy and Angel followed the stream of people, whilst Town Hall officials stood around looking nervous at the gathering crowd. The banqueting room was grand, a wooden ceiling decorated with little sun motifs. The right-hand wall had two grand fireplaces with wooden surrounds, the left-hand wall was made up of windows. The end wall had two large arched bay windows and the carpet was red with blue flowers. Chairs were set up facing the wall with the fireplaces, indicating a speaker would be standing there. Tables were placed in the two bay windows, with leaflets piled high upon them.

Mrs Pankhurst acknowledged Guy and Angel with a nod and a slight double take, then carried on her conversation with a group of men. The couple made their way to the leaflet table and saw the same magazine with Annie Kenney being arrested on the front, that Mrs Pankhurst had given Angel back in London.

Sarah Clarke came over to Guy and Angel. "It's lovely to see you here Miss Jasmine, Angel, and you too Mr Devereux."

"It is an honour to be here," said Angel shaking Sarah's hand. "Will you point out Henry Towers when he gets here, please?"

"You won't have to wait long, he just walked in with his wife, see that couple over there," Sarah nodded towards the door.

"They are a striking couple indeed," said Angel, Guy nodded.

Henry Towers was one of the taller men in the room, dressed in a black morning suit, black waistcoat, white shirt, black bow tie and a top hat. His wife Letitia was standing slightly behind him, wearing a brown cropped jacket, white blouse and matching brown skirt to her ankles, round her waist was a wide green and brown silk belt. Letitia's hat was brown felt, with a couple of little feathers adorning it. Letitia, whilst much shorter than her husband, held herself very straight and had a confident manner.

"Mrs Towers, Letitia, is a committed suffragette, but I don't think Mr Towers ever will be, I don't know why he is here to be honest," said Sarah.

"Do you think you could introduce me to Mrs Towers please?" asked Angel.

"Of course, follow me." Sarah led the way across the room.

"Mrs Towers, please let me introduce you to Miss Jasmine, our newest recruit." Mrs Towers inclined her head to Angel, who nodded in return. "And this is Mr Devereux. They saved me from going back to prison in London, so I am very grateful to them," said Sarah.

"Very well done, I did hear what you did for our sister here," said Mrs Towers. "We do need as much support as we can get. What we really need is people to put pressure on MPs, I do hope we can get some male support today. Although, between you and me, I don't think it will come from Henry."

Guy moved and positioned himself so that he could hear the conversation between Henry Towers and a man dressed very similarly to him.

"Surprised to see you here Towers," said the man. "I didn't think votes for women was a concern of yours."

"It isn't, Letitia gets involved, but I'm here for business reasons," said Henry Towers smiling.

"How is that factory of yours?" asked the man.

"We will manage," said Henry Towers, slightly irritated. "We are diversifying into different areas, cotton on its own is very Victorian, we need to move with the times, keep the factory modern."

Henry nodded his head and moved away to talk to another man who had just walked in, Guy did not feel as though he could follow him without being obvious, he would have to bide his time.

Everyone began to take their seats, Guy and Angel sat in the back row and listened to Mrs Pankhurst talk about the necessity of putting pressure on politicians to support the cause. She also talked about the need to keep the issue of votes for women in the public eye. Several other people spoke briefly and then the audience got up and began to mingle.

The suffragettes were passionately talking to as many people as they could to get their message across, Henry Towers on the other hand was clearly seeking out certain men to discuss business with. Guy was doing his best to listen to conversations and there was one man in particular that Henry Towers seemed to return to and get into deep in conversation with.

"Who is that man that Towers is talking to?" asked Guy as Sarah walked past holding a stash of leaflets.

"Richard Tenney, another cotton mill owner, but I don't know much else about him," replied Sarah.

Guy positioned himself as near as he could, but the conversation was too quiet for him to hear. The two men's body language was interesting, they were looking around them as they spoke, just a little too much, it was clear that they did not want their conversation overheard.

People started to drift off from the meeting, including Henry and Letitia Towers. Guy and Angel said their goodbyes to the suffragettes and Angel promised to meet them on Monday evening at the Pankhurst's house.

*

"Was that useful?" asked Angel as they made their way back to their hotel. "I suppose we know what the Towers both look like now and I have been formally introduced to Mrs Towers."

"Henry was talking to another factory owner, Richard Tenney, they definitely did not want anyone hearing what they had to say, but that is really about all we have to go on."

"So, we need to find out more about Richard Tenney too?"

"We just need something that we can threaten to expose, some criminal activity, anything that will force him to hand over the egg and sign it back to Beatrice, he has to be up to something criminal, surely." Guy pursed his lips in thought. "After all he definitely stole the egg from Beatrice Waibel, if he did that, then he must have few morals and I bet he doesn't bat an eyelid at committing crimes to make money."

"I agree, but I would also bet that he is good at covering his crimes up." Angel led the way up the steps and back into their hotel.

They went into the restaurant for dinner, were shown to a table and gave their order, then began devising a plan for the following day.

"Right, so we are gonna visit the factories tomorrow and see how close they are to each other." Guy put his spoon down, having finished his mushroom soup.

"Absolutely, and see the lay of the land, how close they are to the canals for example," said Angel, dabbing her mouth on a napkin as she too finished her soup.

The waiter took their bowls away.

"If we can, we need to overhear conversations, find out what it was that prompted the very shifty discussions at the town hall," said Guy, smiling at the waiter as a plate of liver and bacon was laid before him. "My grandparents love this, oh well, wish me luck, I'm going in."

"I had liver and bacon before," said Angel. "During a training event, we all spent time in 1939, just before the war broke out, I quite liked it." Angel smiled as Guy paused and looked at her in astonishment.

"You went to 1939? Why?"

"Like I said it was a training event."

"Where were you?"

"London, I'm UK based."

"Of course, silly me." Guy shook his head and tucked into his dinner.

Chapter 14 – Monday 3rd November 1913

In the library Guy and Angel, back in their ordinary clothes, located the Trade Directory for Manchester and found out where the two factories were. The Towers' factory was on the Rochdale Canal in Jersey Street and the Tenney's factory was nearby, also on the canal in Redhill Street.

Angel pursed her lips in thought and nodded her head. "We need to split up."

"I'm just not sure that's a good idea after last time," said Guy, still traumatised from being kidnapped and ending up in France in the seventeenth century.

"We need to follow two people, it makes sense," Angel was determined, "and they are only round the corner from each other. We can get twice as much undercover work done if we split up."

"I know it makes sense," Guy sighed his

resignation to Angel's idea. "I'm just a fish out of water in 1913. But, if you insist, I'll take Henry Towers, I don't think he would recognise me if he saw me, but you were talking to his wife and he might remember you."

"Good idea, I will take the Tenney factory then, we can meet up in a pub round there at an agreed time," Angel linked arms with Guy. "You will be fine, we've been here over a week now, if you feel uncomfortable make your way back to the pub immediately."

Guy smiled and nodded, still unsure about being apart from Angel, whilst he was in the past.

*

The smoke was rising from the chimney at one end of the Towers' factory. It was not the biggest factory by far, but it was still imposing. Dirty redbrick, a ground floor and three more stories above, rows of windows on each floor and the canal ran along the back of the factory. Guy walked around the building, a large wooden entrance door was busy with men, women and children coming and going.

Across the road from the factory were several rows of redbrick terraced houses. Guy crossed over to get a better look at where the workers lived. The houses faced each other across a cobbled street, the backyards were small with a little shed, which Guy guessed to be the outside toilet, he shivered thinking about that prospect, it was cold enough in November, let alone when the snow arrived. The backyards also faced each other across a small, cobbled alleyway, where three boys were having a kickabout with a very battered and flat old ball.

"Do you want to join us mister?" shouted one of the boys.

"He might be from the school board Billy," hissed his friend loud enough for Guy to hear.

"He's too young for that," replied his friend.

"I'm not from the school board, but I would like to ask you some questions about the Towers' factory," said Guy smiling to reassure the boys. The battered old ball landed at Guy's feet and he kicked it back. "Were any of you at the United match on Saturday?"

"Wilf was," said Billy.

"Goals at the start and the end, Liverpool were never in it," Wilf punched the air and kicked an imaginary ball.

"Great game," agreed Guy.

"You speak funny," Wilf laughed screwing his face up.

"I'm from London," replied Guy in explanation.

"Oh, wow, what's it like? I'd love to go there

one day," said Billy. "John's Uncle Mick moved there, didn't he John, but we haven't heard from him, is it safe there?"

"It's similar to Manchester, very busy, less factories but there are still some chimneys puffing away. I'm sure John's uncle is safe and well, just working hard."

"Why aren't you at school by the way?" asked Guy.

"No point," said John. "We'll all be twelve soon, so we can start work in't factory just after Christmas."

"Me ma's still saying I've to be an 'alf-timer," Wilf looked downcast.

"A half-timer? What's that?" asked Guy.

"I've to work in factory in't morning, then go to school in't afternoon. Me older brother did it till he were thirteen, he were so tired, he just slept at 'is desk. It's a waste of time, might as well be in't factory," Wilf shrugged his shoulders.

Guy was aghast looking at the three eleven-year-old boys in front him, wearing raggedy trousers, waistcoats and jackets, with boots that had seen better days and were too big for them. In the twenty-first century they would be in Year 7, learning about the Battle of Hastings and joining the school football club, wearing decent football boots, certainly ones that fitted. Instead, they were having a kick about in a back street, waiting to start work in a factory, maybe working eight or ten hours a day. Guy felt a sudden, and familiar, wave of emotion looking at lads in front of him, tears stung at the back of his eyes, he looked away to the factory over the road and tried to compose himself, before carrying on the conversation.

"Wanna be in goal?" said Wilf, indicating two large stones that represented goal posts.

"Go on then, why not." Guy took up his position between the goalposts, with the alleyway disappearing into the distance behind him.

The boys had a quick meeting and then began their onslaught on Guy, squealing and groaning when he made a save, cheering with delight when they scored and passing the ball to each other strategically to defeat him.

Guy ran down the alleyway to retrieve the ball and had a further awful thought, these boys would turn twelve at the start of 1914, that meant they would be sixteen at the start of 1918, they may well end up in a trench in France or Belgium if they lied about their age, and many did. Even if they escaped the First World War, they would be young enough to be drafted into the Second World War. Guy walked back towards John, Wilf and Billy with a heavy heart, the boys were still celebrating their latest goal and were chuffed with their efforts. Smiling at their success he kicked the ball for the boys to begin their next attack, their future did not bear thinking about.

After half an hour, they all collapsed on the cobbles laughing.

"What does thee want to ask us about Towers?" said Wilf.

"What do you know about Henry Towers?" said Guy still trying to catch his breath.

"Does thee work for him?" said Wilf eyeing Guy suspiciously.

"No, not all, I'm not a spy or anything, if that's what you are worried about."

"Not much to say," said Billy, "me mam says he'd better off letting Mrs Towers run t'factory. She reckons that Towers in't a great businessman."

"Me da says the same," agreed Wilf. "Towers an't got a clue, we are losing a lot of trade to other factories, me da is worried for his job."

"Aye, those special deliveries don't seem to help much either," said John. "That's why me Uncle Mick moved to London, to help with Towers' special deliveries."

"Special deliveries?" asked Guy.

"Aye, sometimes we get a special raw cotton delivery from Egypt, but the special raw cotton has to go to London, we don't process it here, apparently we can't, no idea why, this is Manchester, Cottonopolis," said John, trying to bounce the very flat ball.

"There's a special cotton delivery this evening, it comes from Liverpool, then it has to be unloaded and moved straight onto a train to London. It's important cotton," said Billy. "Me da has to go in tonight to help."

Guy nodded and grabbed the ball from John, getting a bit of bounce out of it. "It must be very special indeed."

The boys stood up ready to resume their game and Guy followed their lead but decided it was time he left to meet Angel.

"Well lads, I need to go and meet my friend, but it has been a pleasure to talk to you." He put his hand in his pocket and felt for his change, he gave them all a penny each. "Go and get something to eat, you need to keep your strength up."

"Thank you," they all yelled in unison, jumping up and scampering off with their ball,

Guy sat back down and wiped a few tears from his eyes, putting his head between his legs he let the tears flow more freely. Breathing deeply and trying to calm his emotions, he felt blessed to be alive in the twenty-first century and not facing a future working ten hours a day in a factory, followed by going to war, maybe twice. He wiped his eyes on his hanky and stood up, going off in search of Angel.

*

"What did you find out?" said Angel, opening the door of the Cross Keys, a little redbrick pub, with green window frames and doors, on the corner of a junction further down Jersey Street.

"Quite a bit, I think I have a lead actually," said Guy following Angel into the dark and smoky pub.

They got a lemonade each, Guy still marvelling at the marbles in the neck of the bottles, and sat at a little round table in the corner of the pub.

"You go first," said Guy, taking a sip of his lemonade.

"Tenney gets special deliveries and there is one tonight. I overheard some women talking about how their husbands had to go back to work tonight, no choice and they didn't think they'd be paid extra either," Angel paused to have sip of her lemonade.

"Same," said Guy. "There is a special delivery coming from Egypt tonight, via Liverpool of course. The delivery is very special raw cotton from Egypt that can't be processed here apparently, it has to go straight to London on a train."

"It must be very special cotton," said Angel puzzled, why on earth can't it be processed here,

Manchester is the cotton capital of the UK at this time, surely. Why London?"

"It's not cotton," said Guy smiling with an expression that said, *I know something you don't know*. "Well, there might be some cotton, but it will be hiding what the shipment really is."

"What is it?"

"Ancient Egyptian artefacts," said Guy confidently.

"Really, how did you find that out?"

"I didn't, I'm guessing, but hear me out. Why are they sending cotton to London? As you said, look at the amount of factories here in Manchester, if they can't deal with the cotton here, no one can."

"That's a good point," agreed Angel, "but how did you make the leap to ancient artefacts?"

"In the present there's a big movement to give artefacts back to their place of origin, the place they were stolen from. Egypt had loads of items stolen, many ended up in private collections or museums in England." Pausing triumphantly, Guy looked very confident with his conclusion. "I'm sure of it. I'm sure they are smuggling artefacts in, disguised as a cotton import, robbed grave goods from the tombs just being found. I don't even think they've found Tutankhamun at this point, so they must be opening up new tombs all the time."

"That's a brilliant name, Tutankhamun, I'd like to meet him," said Angel.

"What?" Guy felt suddenly jealous of the teenage Egyptian pharaoh who died aged nineteen.

"He sounds interesting," replied Angel, knowing nothing about him other than his name and the fact he was Egyptian.

"He wasn't," said Guy. "Anyway, it won't be his grave goods that have been stolen, not yet."

"Ok, how are we going to prove your theory? Should we get a camera and take photos?" suggested Angel.

"I don't think that will work, I thought about that, the shipment is coming this evening, it will be dark, and we'd need a flash. The flash would draw attention to us and even then, if we got away with it, the photos wouldn't be brilliant. I also think the cameras will be too difficult to use."

"Compared to your Smartphone," laughed Angel.

"Definitely. We can't use that can we?" asked Guy knowing the answer. Angel shook her head. "I think we are just going to have to try and get a glimpse of the special delivery and confront Henry Towers with a description," said Guy, taking a big sigh.

"Oh no, I have the suffragette meeting

tonight," said Angel. "I won't go, this is too important."

"No don't cancel, go, we might still need the help of the Pankhurst's and their friends, don't let them down. Anyway, it will be easier for me to conceal myself if I'm on my own."

"You didn't want to be on your own earlier?" said Angel. "Are you sure?"

"I know I didn't, but life could be worse, much worse," said Guy, reflecting on his conversation with the three boys that morning. "Shall we get some lunch, gotta keep our strength up."

*

The canal towpath was lit up by the light from the factories, but Guy kept to the dark areas, hoping he was out of sight in the evening gloom. A barge had arrived at the Towers' factory and wooden crates were being winched up and onto carts, carefully guided by the men who knew the procedures, nothing really looked to be out of place. A slightly bigger horse and cart were waiting patiently to one side, the drivers were two very burley men. Guy decided to keep an eye on them.

Half an hour passed, and Guy shivered in the shadows watching the flurry of action in front of him. The men came to the last wooden crate, it was bigger than the rest and appeared to be heavier too, judging by the number of men needed to steer it.

Guy felt hopeful that he was right about this, he needed to be ready to run. The crate was loaded onto the larger cart, as Guy had suspected it would be and the two drivers immediately sprang into action, the horses responded and the cart left the scene, heading south in the direction of London Road railway station.

Keeping to the dark areas and out of sight, Guy followed the cart, which slowed down in Redhill Street and was joined by another pulling out from the Tenney factory. The two carts wove their way through the streets and over the cobbles, unaware that they were being followed. Guy was not enjoying running on the cobbles in his 1913 boots, he was used to specialised running shoes, not even expensive ones but so much better than his current footwear. He hoped he wouldn't turn an ankle on the cobbles, they were not exactly even.

Ten minutes later the carts arrived at London Road station, with Guy still running in the shadows behind. He followed the carts as they made their way down the platform to the loading area besides the open topped cargo carriages. The station was busy with trains arriving and leaving, people were bustling along and rushing to get on a train, carriage doors opening and closing added to the noise of the steam engines whistling in the cavernous station.

Watching through the smoke, Guy saw the

crates winched onto the open top carriage, the men from the carts he had just followed made sure everything was secure, one man from each cart made their way onto the train itself. The other men left with their two carts, whilst Guy stood on the platform, amid the smoke and people rushing onto the train; he was going to have to make a decision quickly and he knew it.

The time for the train to depart got nearer, the platform emptied as great plumes of smoke began to cloud the station. Glancing around nervously and without thinking for too long, Guy ran into the smoke and jumped on board the open carriage with the special delivery crates, he laid flat on his stomach on top of the crate and hoped he had not been seen, his breathing was heavy as he awaited to find out his fate. The train whistled and pulled away into the dark Manchester night, Guy relaxed, he felt reassured that his whereabouts was safe for now.

Getting his breath back, adrenalin pumping through his veins and glad that he was still warm from his earlier run, Guy jumped down off the crate and sat leaning against it, looking around wondering what to do next. The two special crates were alongside each other, and Guy was sat in between them. Beyond the special crates were several smaller ones, some piled on top of each other. Feeling the floor with his hand, Guy got the impression that this carriage had been used to transport coal in the not-too-distant past.

It wasn't long before the train was in open countryside and Guy was crawling around in the coal dust looking for something to lift the lid on one of the special delivery crates, but he couldn't see or feel anything that might help him. He tried using his hands, but the lid was nailed down, Guy needed something to give him leverage and lift the lid. He continued crawling around in case any tools had been left behind, but the carriage was devoid of anything useful.

The cold air was having an impact on Guy now, he began to shiver as the train chugged into the night. The train was pulling him further and further away from Angel, this gave him a sinking feeling in the pit of his stomach, but there will be trains back to Manchester, he thought, reassuring himself that he could do this task and feeling in his pocket to check he had some money on him.

Crawling over to the smaller crates in the carriage, Guy tried to lift the lid on one of them, wondering if there was anything inside that might be useful. The wood was thinner on these crates and one of the nails was lose, Guy was able to prise open the first crate, but it contained only rolls of material. As he tried to reseal the lid, a chunk of wood splintered off, cutting Guy's hand a little, enough to make him wince. He wrapped his handkerchief around his hand and tied it to stem any blood, then turned his attention to another small crate, the lid wouldn't budge. Guy slumped down beside it.

Shutting his eyes, Guy felt panic rising inside him, his heart was racing, and he definitely couldn't think straight.

"Deep breaths Devereux, come on, deep breaths." Guy opened his eyes, the night sky appeared to be closing in on him as the steam clouds fluttered in the breeze above his head.

Shutting his eyes Guy remembered the grounding technique he used in the Channel in 1648. What could he touch and feel? The hanky on his sore hand, coal dust on the floor. Cold air on his face. What could he taste? Smoke and coal dust – yuk. What could hear? The train chugging. The wind rushing by. A train whistling. What could he smell? Coal dust and smoke? He opened his eyes. What could he see? Not a lot in the dim moonlight except that piece of wood that had cut his hand.

Puffing his cheeks and wondering what to do next, he realised that the wood had broken off into a point.

"That might just do it," he said to no one in particular.

Guy took the wedge of wood and rammed it in between the lid and the box of one of the special crates. The train whistled as he did so, making him jump out of skin and his heart pound. He looked at the crate and the wood had indeed caught just under the lid; he pushed with all his might and slid the wedge of wood further to try and separate the two. After a few minutes of wiggling and sliding the wedge of wood around, the lid became loose as a nail wobbled.

His hands were very cold and one was quite sore but he had to push on, now he had an edge loose it made it easier to work a couple more nails free, eventually Guy had the corner of one of the crates free from nails, he paused, exhausted and shivering.

"The sooner I see this, the sooner I can get off," said Guy into the night, before continuing to free the lid from nails along one side of the crate.

Lifting the lid as much as he could he put an arm in and began to feel around, he felt a lot of sacking and was able to squeeze it, giving him the impression that it did indeed contain raw Egyptian cotton. He rummaged in between the squidgy sacks and pushed his arm down as far as it would go, he could feel a sack at the bottom of the crate that was hard, it felt as though it contained something made of stone.

"I knew it, I flippin' knew it," said Guy trying to get an angle on it and pull the sack into his moonlit view. Finally, he pushed both arms into the crate and dragged the hard sack through the soft ones.

"Oh, to have my phone now," sighed Guy,

wishing he had access to a torch and a camera. He couldn't tell if the shivering was fear, cold, or excitement that he could be holding the answer to getting the Faberge egg back to the present day and, more importantly, back to Barbara for little Chloe's operation.

He wriggled the sack so that the top was presenting itself, even though he couldn't see it very well in the gloom of the night. With all his strength he ripped the sack apart and began to feel about inside. The stone object was smooth and shaped like something, Guy couldn't tell what until he came to something he was sure were two pointy ears.

"A cat, it's a cat, it has to be a cat, surely!"

He continued to rummage in the sack and found what felt as though it was a small statue, maybe in the shape of an Egyptian mummy.

"Am I doing that thing where your mind just plays tricks on you?" Guy asked himself.

At that moment the train began to slow down, whistles blew and Guy realised that they were approaching a station. As the train ground to a halt lamplight flooded the open carriage. Guy instinctively left the crate, pushing the lid back in place and crawled over to the smaller crates, hiding behind them, as they appeared to have nothing to do with Towers and Tenney.

Just as well he did. The two men he had seen

get on the train from the carts suddenly peered over the top of the open carriage. Guy's heart was beating so loud, he was sure they would hear it. Would the two men notice anything was out of place, had he left everything as it should look? Where was that wedge of wood?

"All good Mick?" said one of the men.

"Aye, all's well and sound, gonna be a long night though."

"Yeah, let's get some kip in before we get to London."

The men pleased with what they saw, jumped back down to the platform, Guy heard a carriage door shut and he hoped it was the men getting back inside the third-class carriage next to the crates.

Knowing it was a good opportunity, with light coming from the platform, Guy scurried along the floor back to the crate and lifted the lid. He found the sack he had been rummaging in and pulled it up to the top of the crate, lifting it into the light. The latest cloud of smoke cleared to reveal what Guy had suspected all along, it was a statue of a black cat, clearly in the Egyptian style he remembered from primary school lessons, it had a long back and pointed ears, it was indeed very distinct. He quickly pulled the little statue to the top of the sack; it was a blue Egyptian mummy with black hieroglyphics scrawled along the body.

He didn't have time to find out what else was hidden in the crate, as the train was puffing and whistling in its pre departure ritual.

"I knew it, I just knew it," said Guy as a guard blew his whistle and the train started to move slowly.

With a momentary flash back to the time he jumped off a ship in the Channel a few months earlier. Guy positioned himself to jump off a moving train. He knew he needed that bravery and confidence now, but it was dark and he didn't really know what he was jumping into or onto.

More smoke provided the coverage he needed, Guy leapt up to the side of the carriage, as the train approached the end of the platform, he jumped off it. He hit the platform, landing on his feet, once again wishing for trainers with some sort of shock absorbency. The train chugged on, unaware of the extra passenger that had just left, and Guy was alone on a dark train station, hiding behind a building, not having a clue where he was.

Even in the dark night sky Guy could make out the shadows of chimneys, and he could certainly still smell the industrial air, he couldn't be that far from Manchester. Ensuring that he wasn't seen by the guards, Guy weaved and bobbed his way out of the station, as he hadn't had time to purchase a ticket back in Manchester. He looked around in the shadowy lights and realised the train had just crossed a huge railway viaduct, one he had crossed many times with his dad going to and from Old Trafford, he was in Stockport.

Now outside the station, he realised that what he actually needed was a train back to Manchester, so he went back into the station and looked at the train timetable on the wall. He saw that the next train back wasn't until the morning. Guy nodded, he didn't think there would be another train tonight and he had prepared himself for that. He left the station once more and made his way down into the town, the giant Stockport Viaduct looming above him gave an eerie feel to the moonlit streets, which echoed with a distant horse and cart clip clopping along.

The Railway pub was the nearest place Guy could see, it was not yet closing time, so he brushed himself free of coal dust as best he could and went in to ask for directions to a hotel. The smell of smoke and alcohol was overwhelming as he walked across the pub, and very reminiscent of the French fishing village he had found himself in back in 1648. The customers were standing around in groups on the sawdust covered floor, chatting and laughing, there were no tables or benches here, only a few barstools around the edges. The customers were mainly men, and many were not a lot older than Guy. Putting the morbid thought of World War One *pals battalions* to the back of his head once more, he approached the bar.

"Hello, I wondered if you could help me? I need a hotel for the night," Guy shouted to the barman, to make himself heard.

The barman turned away and beckoned a woman over, she was middle aged, sturdy and didn't look like she would take any nonsense from anyone. Guy guessed correctly that she was landlady.

"Eh chuck, were ye wanting a room for the night? Just you?" she asked.

"That's right," said Guy. "Do you know anywhere?"

"Well, I do rightly know of somewhere, I have two rooms spare, and you'd be very welcome to one of 'em pet."

"I'll take it," Guy was not bothered what state the room was in, he just wanted to sleep.

He paid his money and was shown to a little room, that was pleasant enough, it had an iron bedstead with a green quilted eiderdown on top, washstand, a wardrobe and the toilet was down the hallway, he made use of that first then went back to the room and washed as best he could.

It was only when he sat down on the bed that he thought of Angel, she would be back at their hotel in Manchester by now and worried about him. Still there was nothing he could do, there were no text messages to be sent or video calls to be had; he would get the first train back to Manchester in the morning and hopefully see Angel at breakfast.

Thinking he would find it difficult to sleep, Guy pulled back the sheets, blankets and quilt, he thought the day's events would be racing through his head and the confrontation with Henry Towers to come would play on his mind. He was, however, very wrong, he undressed to his underwear, glad of the Long Johns because the room was cold and he got into the creaky bed. Within five minutes he was sound asleep and too exhausted to dream.

Chapter 15 – Tuesday 4th November 1913

The water in the washstand jug was freezing, Guy shivered as the skin on his arms became full of goosebumps. He was grateful of the water though and so with a quick wash and brush up, Guy left the pub in Stockport at half past six in the morning, having slept very well under the cosy quilt and blankets. He retraced his steps to the train station and by seven o'clock he was on his way back to Manchester, in a third class compartment this time, with a ticket and a reasonably comfortable seat.

By eight o'clock Guy was in his hotel dining room in Manchester eating breakfast and looking out for Angel. He was desperate to tell her about the events of the night before, as they now had something concrete that they could confront Henry Towers about. For the first time Guy felt as though they might get the Faberge egg back and be able to return to the twenty-first century with a gift for Barbara.

A rush of sadness passed through him, as much as Guy wanted to get home and feel safe with his family, Angel was not there, for him, she lived in the past and he could not see her in the present. Would he ever see her again after this trip? He had no idea, but he did know that he would think about her for the rest of his life, how could he ever forget such a strong, confident, risk-taking woman. Or angel. Was that the same thing? He didn't know.

The wall clock in its wooden case, with its pendulum keeping time, ticking away the moments, told Guy that it was quarter to nine, where was Angel? She should be down for breakfast by now, it finished at nine. Guy's thoughts switched from his adventures to Angel's, she had been at a suffragette meeting, suddenly there was a sinking feeling in the pit of his stomach.

Drinking the last of his English Breakfast tea, Guy left the dining area and made his way up to Angel's room, which was three doors along from his own. He knocked on the door and called her name, there was no answer, he banged harder on the door, much to the annoyance of a couple returning from breakfast. Perhaps she was in the shared bathroom down the hall, he knocked on that door and was met with a gruff voice telling him to clear off. The nagging thought of Angel being with the suffragettes would not go away.

Where was she? Was she ill? Had she just stayed at the Pankhurst's? No, she wouldn't have done that. Guy's mind was racing as he made his way back to the hotel foyer.

At the reception desk Guy waited patiently as a couple checked-in, trying to calm his nerves, the check-in seeming to take forever, finally he spoke to the man on duty.

"Hello, I'm Mr Devereux in room sixteen, my friend, Miss Jasmine, is in room ten but I can't seem to find her this morning. Do you know if she left the hotel already?"

"Her key is here sir; it was here when I began my shift at six o'clock. Perhaps she stayed somewhere else last night sir," the man smiled. "Does she have friends in Manchester?"

"Not really, maybe," said Guy, the sinking feeling in his stomach spreading across his chest, arms and legs. "She didn't leave any messages for me I suppose?"

"I'm sorry sir, there's nothing here."

"Thank you for your help," said Guy turning away and looking around the hotel foyer in the hope that Angel would just appear.

He walked to the sofas and took a seat; Guy wanted some time to collect his thoughts. He would have to go to the Pankhurst's house and start there, if something had happened suffragette wise, they would know, he was pushing the thought of Angel setting fire to a post box out of his mind. As he stood up to leave, the man on reception called him back over.

"Mr Devereux, there is a message for you, just arrived."

"For me, thank you," said Guy with some trepidation. He took the envelope and returned to the sofa, he needed to be seated, his hands were shaking as he opened it.

Dear Mr Devereux

It is with regret that I must inform you Miss Jasmine was arrested last night with three other sisters. She is currently in Newton Street Police Station and will likely appear in court this morning.

In the name of the cause

Votes for Women

Guy stared at the note, not really in disbelief, he knew this would happen, 1913 was a peak time for suffragette activity. He felt sure Angel would have just got caught up in something, he did not think that she would really set fire to a post box or cricket pavilion, but she might not have known exactly what was about to happen.

Feeling for his phone in his pocket, irritated that it was not there, and he did not have access to an online map *app*, Guy went back over to the reception man. "Excuse me, where is Newton Street?"

"Ah, the police station," the man rolled his eyes. "One of those suffragettes is she? She'd be better off with some of the other groups fighting for the vote, rather than smashing windows and setting things on fire."

"Thank you for your advice, but I need to get to the police station urgently," said Guy politely.

The man drew him a map and Guy looked at it hurriedly.

"Oh yes, out towards the Etihad, that area," said Guy without thinking and referencing Manchester City's Stadium, which would not be built for a very long time.

"Towards the 'what' sir?" said the man, puzzled.

"Oh, nothing, ignore me, thank you for your help." With that Guy rushed off outside into the damp Manchester air, hoping he could get to the police station before Angel was taken to court.

*

There was no mistaking the police station, it was a redbrick building with a bright blue door and matching window frames, above the entrance was a blue police lamp. Guy was relieved to see the large blue doors were open as he stopped on the pavement out of breath from running. Two police constables left the building, their black uniform and silver buttons not totally unrecognisable to twenty-first century eyes, apart from the frock capes needed to keep them dry.

The reception area was small, with a wooden L-shaped desk and seat that looked like a church pew. The policeman on reception was talking to someone behind him, so Guy had to wait patiently, but then he overheard part of the conversation, and it began to make him feel anxious.

"Four cells they're taking up, it's ridiculous, that's what it is, as if they will ever get the vote by vandalising property and burning buildings to the ground. They're all in't magistrates court this morning, more time wasted, just take them straight to prison and let us get on with catching real criminals. In fact tis a real shame we don't just send 'em all off to Australia like we used to do in't olden days."

Rant over the police officer turned to face Guy. "Yes sir, PC Norris, how can I help?"

"My friend, Miss Jasmine, she is one of the women that you are talking about, is she still here?"

The policeman looked at the clock, Guy followed his gaze, it was quarter to ten.

"Court starts at ten, they'll be waiting to go

in by now."

"Oh no, where is the court? Is it far?" Guy didn't fancy another run on the Manchester cobbles.

"It's here in the same building. At least we don't have to waste our efforts transporting time wasters across Manchester."

Guy ignored the policeman's comments. "Can I see her before she goes in? I need to talk to her urgently."

"Not a chance, but thee can sit in't public gallery and listen to the whole sorry tale of how they tried to burn down Holy Name Church last night."

"What? Angel, Miss Jasmine, she wouldn't do that, you've made a mistake."

"We've not. All four of them were in that church, smashing up statues and ready to set fire to pews."

"I'm telling you, Miss Jasmine would one hundred percent not have been doing that, you don't understand," said Guy, slightly raising his voice in panic.

"I'm telling thee, that she were there. Now does thee want to go to the public gallery or not? If thee does, thee is going to have to calm down."

"Yes, I do, I'm sorry," said Guy, trying to control his frustration. "How do I get in?

*

All Guy could hear was his heart beating as he took his seat in the public gallery. Looking around at the very grand, although small magistrates' courtroom, he felt as though he was in a bad dream, his head swimming with visions of Angel running amok in the church. He knew this couldn't be and that there had to be an explanation, but how Angel was going to get out of this he had no idea. Perhaps she would create her wind tunnel and disappear, then come back for him. But did she need to be in the open air to create the wind tunnel? He didn't know, he had never asked.

He was sat facing the bench, where the magistrates would be seated very soon. A large clock was mounted on the wall behind the bench, very similar to the one in the hotel dining room; wooden case, brass pendulum, ticking ominously in the background. There were desks in front of the bench. In the centre of the room was the dock, a large wooden box for the accused to stand in, with an iron railing behind it. The public gallery was behind the dock, perhaps the iron railing was there to protect those in the dock thought Guy.

A court clerk in his smart black suit asked everyone to rise and the three magistrates walked in, taking their seats on the bench. All three were men with varying lengths of silver beards and bald heads with side whiskers. Guy was reminded of

Father Ciaran back in his real life. The magistrates were dressed in black suits, black waistcoats and white shirts, with a black bow tie. Guy though they looked like vultures as they craned their necks over the bench.

The court usher brought in an old man and led him to the dock. He was accused of being drunk and disorderly and urinating up a statue. He admitted his guilt, was fined and led away. The next person to be brought in was a young woman, clearly heavily pregnant, she was dressed in dirty and ripped clothes, that would have offered her no respite from the cold outside. She was charged with stealing bread, not having any money to pay a fine, she was sentenced to thirty days in prison, Guy wondered if she had wanted to go to prison to give birth, he hoped a charity would find her and support her.

Next up in front of the magistrates was the first of the four suffragettes, she was brought in and placed in the dock. Guy did not recognise her.

"Miss Mary Crowley, you have been charged with vandalism to Holy Name Church and conspiracy to set fire also to Holy Name Church," declared the middle magistrate. "How do you plead?"

"Guilty, sir. Guilty of fighting for the cause. Guilty of raising awareness of the injustice that is women not having the vote." Mary was upright, confident and clearly proud of her role in the fight for women's suffrage.

"You are sentenced to six months in gaol," replied the magistrate after nodding at the other two men.

"And will I be treated as a political prisoner?" asked Mary.

"You know you will not be given that title Miss Crowley, you have been here before."

"Then you know what will happen, I will refuse food," said Mary firmly.

"Then you too, know what will happen, Miss Crowley, we will release you and rearrest you until your sentence is complete. Is that all?"

Mary glared at the magistrate as the policeman snapped on some handcuffs and led her away. Guy watched the spectacle feeling very lightheaded, his heart thumping and his hands unable to stay still. At least she would not be force fed, but the Cat and Mouse Act was also brutal, it made the women very weak. Guy remembered Sarah's exhaustion in St. James Park the first time he met her. Was Sarah here this morning?

The second suffragette was brought to the dock, much smaller than Mary Crowley and looking quite timid.

"Miss Cecilia Turner, you have been charged with vandalism to Holy Name Church and conspiracy to set fire also to Holy Name Church, how do you plead?" asked the magistrate, a little kindlier this time.

"Guilty," whispered Cecilia.

"Louder for the court to hear please Miss Turner," said the magistrate on the left.

Cecilia took a deep breath. "Guilty your honour," she said, her voice shaking.

"Miss Turner, this is your first offence, you must think clearly whether or not this cause of action is for you. You are sentenced to three months in prison."

"The cause is for me sir, it's an injustice, I will proudly serve my time as a political prisoner," Cecilia had found her voice.

"Then you too will find yourself at the mercy of the Cat and Mouse," said the magistrate to the right, irritated by Cecilia's words.

Once again the handcuffs were snapped on and the suffragette was led away to await transportation to gaol. The three magistrates sighed and looked at each other, rolling their eyes and shuffling paper, clearly annoyed at having to deal with suffragettes fighting for their cause.

The cry of "votes for women" rung loud across the courtroom, making everyone jump, including the three magistrates. Guy was relieved to see Sarah Clarke being led across to the dock and smiled as she continued her chant, undeterred by the rough treatment from the policeman holding her.

"Miss Sarah Clarke, you have been charged with vandalism to Holy Name Church and conspiracy to set fire also to Holy Name Church," said the magistrate, staring at Sarah and holding her gaze. "How do you plead?"

"Guilty, guilty of fighting for votes for women and proud to do so," shouted Sarah across the room to the three magistrates. "But you need to know this," she added.

"We need to know what?" said the magistrate on the left, raising his eyebrows at his colleagues and looking back to Sarah.

"Miss Jasmine, she was with us, but she had not been involved in the discussions yesterday evening, she was not aware of the actions that were about to take place when we walked into Holy Name Church. It would be an injustice to convict her. She was upset when we smashed statues and tried to prevent us from causing damage. Maybe in the future she will join us, who knows, but on this occasion, she was not involved."

Sarah looked around and smiled at Guy in the public gallery, he nodded and smiled back, he knew it, but would the magistrates believe it.

"Thank you, Miss Clarke, you are sentenced to six months in prison. As you are from London, we shall be checking with our colleagues there and if you are already part way through a sentence, this one will be added on."

Sarah did not reply, she held her head high and wrists out for the handcuffs. Once applied she was led away, still chanting "votes for women," Guy wondered if all her sentences would be finished before war broke out in August 1914.

Angel was brought into the dock, she looked around and saw Guy in the public gallery, following a wry smile in his direction she returned her attention to the magistrates.

"Miss Jasmine of no fixed abode, currently staying at the Crown Hotel, Manchester, you have been charged with vandalism to Holy Name Church and conspiracy to set fire also to Holy Name Church, how do you plead?" asked the central magistrate.

"Not guilty sir," said Angel confidently.

"Not guilty, but you were there in the church last night with three other women who have all pleaded guilty to these acts of vandalism. Why should we believe you were any different?"

"I was at the suffragette meeting, that is true and afterwards I was walking back to my hotel with Miss Clarke. The two other suffragettes were someway in front of us, I did not know they had entered the church already. When we got to Holy Name Church, Miss Clarke suggested we go in, I thought we were going in for prayer. I had no idea of the acts that were about to follow." Angel paused and swallowed.

"It caused me great distress to see religious artefacts destroyed, when some cans of liquid were produced, I tried to stop them pouring the liquid onto the pews. I believe women should get the vote, but not at the expense of arson." Angel turned round to Guy as she finished her speech.

"Miss Jasmine," boomed the magistrate on the left, making Angel jump and turn back to face him. "Have you been living on the moon these past months?"

Angel shook her head. "Not exactly, no," she replied.

"Well then, you will know that the small group of women who call themselves suffragettes, will set fire to almost anything to make their point. Many churches across the country have suffered this fate, not to mention other public buildings, golf clubs and cricket pavilions. Women will not get the vote whilst this persists, indeed it shows women to be of irrational thought. So why should we believe that you had no clue that the intention of these women was destruction upon entering the church yesterday evening?"

"Miss Jasmine was not aware of the situation," said a woman's voice from behind Guy. There was an audible gasp across the court room,

Guy turned to see who the posh voice belonged to. He was surprised to see none other than Letitia Towers standing firm and confident in her brown coat trimmed with fur and matching hat.

"This is very irregular, you have not been called as witness," said the middle magistrate.

"It's very irregular that women do not have the vote too," said Letitia Towers undeterred. "Miss Jasmine was not involved in the discussion, she was simply, in the wrong place at the wrong time. She was walking in the same direction; it would have been rude not to walk with someone you had been at a meeting with. If you convict her, it will be an injustice. You have heard the evidence from Miss Clarke yourself."

The courtroom was silent, everyone was still as Letitia Towers sat down, staring hard at the magistrates, not averting her gaze anywhere else. Guy looked from Letitia Towers to the magistrates and back. No one seemed to know what to say for a moment, then the magistrates began to confer.

"Miss Jasmine, we have heard the statement from yourself, the evidence from Miss Clarke and the highly irregular evidence from Mrs Towers," the middle magistrate glared at Letitia. "However, on this occasion we find that we do not have enough evidence to convict you, you are found not guilty and you are indeed free to go."

Sighs of relief sounded around the

courtroom, Guy turned round to say thank you to Letitia Towers for intervening, but she had gone. Angel was being led out of the court, so Guy left the public gallery and made his way back to the reception desk. PC Norris was still on duty and was giving Angel a lecture.

"You need to stay away from those Pankhursts in future, there are thousands of women campaigning for the vote that don't go round smashing things up and causing criminal damage. My sister goes on very peaceful demonstrations, she organises petitions and hands out leaflets. You'd be better off working with them, mark my words."

"Thank you sir, I will take your advice, I promise." Angel put her gloves on and shook PC Norris' hand.

"Shall we go?" said Guy linking arms with Angel and guiding her out, keen to get her away from the police station before the magistrates changed their minds.

Once out into the street they hurried across the road and away from Newton Street at the earliest opportunity, neither said anything as they bustled through the busy streets, not knowing where to begin, each keeping their thoughts to themselves for a few minutes. They arrived back in Piccadilly Gardens and sat on a park bench, pleased for the relative calm of the space.

"I am so sorry, that should not have happened, I genuinely thought we were going into the church to pray," Angel held both of Guy's hands in hers. "Mrs Pankhurst wasn't at the meeting, apparently she has gone to America to raise funds for the cause."

"I wondered why she wasn't in the courtroom," said Guy.

"The meeting was all talk about the bombing of the parks, which will take place soon, not that a date was given. There was no suggestion of setting fire to a church. Although Sarah was in a huddle with Mary and Cecilia all night, but I thought they just had a specific role to play in the park bombings." Angel paused and looked around the gardens. "I didn't even speak to Mrs Towers other than to say hello, I didn't really speak to anyone. I can't believe Mrs Towers did that. Guy, can you say something?"

"It's been a long morning, I'm still recovering, you are not good for my blood pressure Angel." Guy smiled and squeezed Angel's hands. "I'm just glad that you are not on your way to prison, that's all."

"Shall we get something to eat and a hot sweet cup of tea, isn't that supposed to be good for shock." Angel smiled and then noticed Guy's cut hand. "What on earth happened to your hand? Oh, my goodness what happened last night? I'm so rude, I have been so wrapped in myself and my prison situation. Did you find anything out?"

"Let's go to the tea rooms, get something to eat and I will tell you all about my evening, which was traumatic enough, without finding you missing this morning," Guy let out a huge sigh and stood up, pulling Angel with him. They linked arms and walked off across Piccadilly Gardens to find some tea rooms.

*

The waitress brought over a plate of small triangular sandwiches, some ham, some cheese, and laid them on the table. A second waitress gently set down a three-tiered cake stand with lots of gorgeous little cakes just waiting to tempt Guy and Angel. The first waitress returned with a pot of tea, cups, sugar bowl and milk jug, all in the same delicate pink and yellow flowery design.

"Thank you," said Guy and Angel in unison.

"I'm actually ravenous, I don't recommend a police cell breakfast, tiny bowl of what I think was supposed to be cold porridge." They both shuddered at the thought and selected some sandwiches for their plates.

"I say we don't split up again," said Guy, "it's just too stressful. I know we need to keep the suffragettes as contacts, they are useful but...."

"Don't worry Guy, I'm not going to anymore

suffragette meetings, I shall take the advice of the policeman on the desk and join a different suffrage group, one that isn't so militant."

"What do you mean? Do you need to join another group now?" Guy took a bite of his ham sandwich and looked Angel in confusion.

"Oh, not now, I meant after the egg is returned," said Angel reaching for her second cheese sandwich.

"You are taking me back home aren't you?" Guy paused his eating.

"Yes, of course, sorry, I wasn't thinking, I mean after I drop you home. I have some time owing and I thought I might pop back, to see how this all pans out."

"So you jump around in time, like I might jump on a plane and go to Spain or Greece," Guy was pleased she hadn't mentioned Tutankhamun again, then shook his head, he was going mad.

"I suppose you could put it like that, when I'm not working anyway," said Angel. "I feel as though I need to learn more about these women, the suffragists and the suffragettes, what better place to find out than Manchester in 1913. It seems to centre here, what with the Pankhursts, but not just them. All the thousands of women in the mills, the suffragists, the ones that just want the right to vote, so that they can have a say in what happens to their lives."

"You sound like my GCSE History teacher," laughed Guy. "Remember what I told you in London, it is the suffragist Millicent Fawcett whose statue stands in Parliament Square."

"That makes sense now," said Angel as she reached for yet another cheese sandwich. "Being arrested, thrown in a cell and taken to court, really does make you hungry."

Guy laughed. "You go for it. We need to keep our strength up."

"What did you find out?" asked Angel. "And how did you cut your hand?"

"Long story, buckle up, here goes," Guy took a deep breath and recalled the incidents of the previous night.

"You did what?" Angel was horrified as she heard how he jumped onto the open cargo carriage and was carried off into the night.

"It was so frustrating not being able to get the crates open, having come so far and being so close. That's when I cut my hand on a piece of wood. I think I might still have a splinter actually."

"Oooh, I'm good at getting those out," said Angel, "I will have a go later."

"Thanks, I think," said Guy pulling a face. "Anyway, when I did prise the lid open, all I could see were sacks of raw cotton, I had a rummage around and at the bottom of the crate was another sack, when I managed to pull it to the top and look inside, there was a statue, a black cat, clearly Egyptian in style and a smaller statue in the shape of a mummy, with hieroglyphics on it."

Angel gasped and froze with a cream slice in her hand. "You were right, you said that you thought he was importing Egyptian artefacts. Well, that's it then, we have our confrontation." Angel suddenly looked a bit downcast.

"Hey, what's the matter? We should be happy right now."

"It's just that, I really hope Letitia Towers isn't in on this. She went out of her way to speak up for me in the courtroom just now. If she hadn't, I might be on my way to prison."

"I doubt she is aware. She seems like a lady who wants justice to me," said Guy thoughtfully. "But you're right, it would be awful if she was part of Henry Towers' criminal activity. And what would I have done with you in prison?"

"I wouldn't have made it there Guy, I think the wind would have got up at some point," Angel laughed. "Don't worry, I wouldn't have left you here, but I would have been playing my own game of cat and mouse with the Manchester police."

"The thing is Angel, I just don't know all your rules," said Guy sighing as bit into a light and fluffy scone.

"You know more than you need to. Anyway, how did you get off the train and back to Manchester?"

"I jumped off as the train pulled away from the station," said Guy proudly.

"You do like jumping off things don't you," laughed Angel. "What station was it?"

"I was in Stockport, but there were no trains back to Manchester until this morning, so I stayed in a nice little room in a pub."

"So, you didn't know I was missing until this morning," said Angel. "That must have been quite a shock when I didn't turn up for breakfast.

"Do you know what? I wasn't actually that shocked if I'm honest, blooming annoyed, but not shocked."

"We all live and learn I guess, I'm sorry." Angel reached across to squeeze Guy's hand.

"It's not your fault, and no harm has been done, let's just move on," said Guy, turning his hand to squeeze Angel's, before reaching for another small chocolate fairy cake.

When all the cakes and sandwiches were eaten and only a few crumbs remained, the waitress cleared the plates away, leaving Guy and Angel to finish their tea.

"When are we going to confront Henry Towers then?" said Guy.

"I think we should do it tomorrow at breakfast, we know he will be at home then," replied Angel.

Guy laughed and shook his head. "He might be at home, but we don't know where the Towers live."

"Oh no, back to the Pankhursts?" said Angel grimacing.

"No, we will go to the factory and follow him home. If we don't manage it tonight, then we will follow him every night until we find out where he lives."

"You really don't want me going back to the Pankhursts do you?" said Angel drinking the last of her tea.

"No, I flippin' don't, funnily enough," said Guy smiling. "We're on our own now, nearly there."

"He could leave the factory anytime from about four o'clock I reckon, so we'd better get over there," said Angel, indicating to the waitress that they needed the bill by miming a scribble on her hand.

*

As they arrived at Henry Towers' factory, Guy looked across the road to the little back alley where he had played football with John, Wilf and Billy the day before. They were not there but a young woman holding a toddlers' hand was just leaving. Guy felt that the woman and child looked rather underdressed for the cold and windy November afternoon, he exchanged a grimacing glance with Angel.

"We can't fix everything Guy." Angel looked at the woman with pity in her eyes and shivered. "It's awful when you see things that are out of place with your twenty-first century eyes, but we are here to find some lost treasure and return it to the rightful owner. Time will improve the rest."

"If only it did." Guy sighed and shook his head. "Ok, let's locate Towers, and get ready to follow him, how fast can you run?"

"It's not my favourite pastime, especially in these boots on those cobbles, but I will do my best to keep up. Let's hope he doesn't live too far. Or his chauffeur doesn't drive too fast."

"I wonder, can we get in the factory? See if he is still there." Guy walked towards a large arched entrance, where carts were pulling in and out. "I reckon the offices are upstairs."

"We'll soon find out."

The arched entrance led them to a courtyard, which was busy with huge bails of raw cotton being unloaded from carts.

"Crikey, where do we start?" said Guy looking up and down the building. "The offices could be anywhere, and he might not even be in them."

"Look there is a little entrance over there, let's try that." Angel pointed to a door.

The door took them into a maze of corridors, the sounds of the factory machinery very evident, but not in sight.

"We need to get upstairs, can you see any," said Guy, looking around in vain.

"Not stairs but look at that." Angel pointed as she jumped out of the way of a handcart full of raw cotton being pushed towards a huge open lift.

"Might as well then." Guy let Angel walk in front of him and they joined the cart in the lift. The man pushing the cart pulled across the outer door of the lift and then the inner door. Once it clanged shut, he pushed a button and up they went to the top floor. Their destination was reached soon enough and the man opened both doors, Guy and Angel stepped aside to let the cart go first, then followed.

They had arrived on the factory floor, and it was deafening,

"Oh my God," mouthed Guy. "It's really loud."

Angel nodded in agreement, and they shook their heads slowly, opened mouthed in horror as they surveyed the scene before them. The room was so long that they couldn't even see then end, it was packed with different types of machinery, and the ceiling was low. There were windows, but the light didn't seem to be very bright, although it was late afternoon gloom by now anyway. There were metal pillars at regular intervals, supporting the roof and wisps of cotton flying everywhere.

Guy tugged Angel's arm and pointed to the room, indicating they should go in. She nodded, they made their way across the factory floor, choking with the cotton dust and ducking out of the way of anyone who looked like they were in charge.

The workers were so focused on their jobs that they paid little attention to the visitors. Neither did the workers pay any attention to the cotton dust making the air inside the room thick. There seemed to be different stages of the process in different areas, it was difficult to take it all in, the noise making it difficult to think with any clarity.

On one side a couple of girls, whom Guy thought to be younger than him, maybe thirteen or fourteen years old, were working on a series of about ten machines. The machines themselves had large rollers, from which thick ropes of white cotton emerged and were winding their way into a beige coloured can at the front of the machine. Guy felt that one machine alone sounded like ten washing machines all spinning at the same time, with ten machines in a row, that was the noise of a hundred washing machines. It occurred to Guy that no one was wearing ear defenders either.

When the beige cans were full, the girls carried them to some larger red cans that surrounded another machine, maybe sixty to eighty red cans, Guy couldn't tell. The girls swiftly and expertly joined the cotton ropes together and they threaded through to the centre of the machine, Guy couldn't see what happened next, until someone from further along the factory came and took what looked like a giant slab of cotton. Guy turned his attention to the other side of the room, where he could see teenage boys about his age, working in unison, moving a huge frame that had lots of little cotton bobbins spinning round.

Catching each other's eyes, Guy and Angel shrugged, there were no offices here, they nodded and made their way back to the lift, however, on the way Guy noticed a stairwell and pointed to it, so they both hurried towards that, eager to get away from the factory floor. Halfway down the stairwell they stopped to catch their breath and clear their lungs from cotton dust.

"That was horrendous, those poor people," said Angel. "Their life expectancy has to be impacted by the dust, not to mention their hearing."

"What an awful place to work, we learnt about it in Year 8, but I never imagined it to be so loud and dusty." Guy spoke whilst trying to pull flecks of cotton out of his mouth.

Angel shook her head and was trying to dust herself down, the cotton flecks having stuck to her navy outfit, she looked as though a golden retriever had been jumping up and down at her.

"Where now?" Guy craned his neck over the stairs. "These offices could be anywhere."

"Let's just try this floor anyway," said Angel as they reached the second floor. "It's not as noisy as the others."

They followed passages of green and white painted brick, smiling at people hurrying by, walking along with purpose and intent, as though they were supposed to be there and they knew exactly where they were going. Finally, they came to a series of offices, windows and glass doors making it apparent that it was the administration area. Various names were written on the green painted wooden doors, but Henry Towers' name was not one of them.

Then they came to a smarter area, with wood doors that were not painted green, but were trimmed with brass, they both paused before a big window, it was just possible that Henry Towers would recognise them from the previous Sunday at Manchester Town Hall. Managing to position themselves with a good view of the office through the glass in the door, but shielded from view, they could see that Henry Towers was sitting at a large wooden desk with a green and brass lamp and an inkwell set atop it. He was talking to a man who was standing and holding a pile of folders.

Pleased with their surveillance, Guy and Angel nodded to each other and made their way back to the stairwell, running quickly down to the ground floor and out into the courtyard. Both glad of the fresh air, they choked, sneezed and then yawned to try and clear their ears from popping with the noise from the cotton machinery.

"At least we know he hasn't left yet," said Guy. "Let's get in position over the road, we can hide in the alleyway."

"Good idea, come on, let's get away from this dreadful place." They crossed the road and installed themselves in the alleyway, which had the added bonus of giving them a bit of protection from the cold wind.

"I was just thinking," said Guy, "when we get the Faberge egg, because hopefully we will, let's be positive."

"Absolutely we will." Angel nodded in agreement.

"Are you going to deliver me straight back to the twenty-first century?"

"If I do, you will be in Manchester."

"Hmm, not ideal, because if you are going to deliver me back to the moment we left the twenty-first century, I will never get back in time for that roast dinner," Guy laughed. "Not unless, can you deliver me back earlier in the day on the 23rd October?"

"No, I can't deliver you back until a minute after you left with me. You can't go back in time in your own timeline, because then there would be two of you and that isn't good, trust me on that." Angel held Guy's arm and looked into his eyes to make her point.

"I see, that makes sense. Do you think we should go back to London at least?"

Angel nodded. "I think so, preferably Chalk Hill, an area where we know what it looks like in the twenty-first century. If I take you back to the twenty-first century in Manchester, I might drop you onto a road, or the top of a building, or tramline, something that wasn't there in 1913. It would be too dangerous."

"Yeah, defo, I don't want to be deposited on the Manchester ring road or anything." Guy shuddered. "Ok, once we have the egg, we will go straight back to the station and get on the next train to London, that's a plan then."

"We can take the underground to Liverpool

Street and get on a train to Chalk Hill, then I will drop you back to your own time, on the 23rd October, one minute after you left. Well hopefully, I've done the training anyway." Angel grinned. "Although that didn't always go according to plan. Long story."

They both laughed, but the laugh faded as they looked at each other, realising the adventure might soon be over.

"Will I see you again?" asked Guy quietly.

"Never say never," replied Angel, "but you know, you have a whole life to get on with. That fancy dress Hallowe'en party for one thing."

"I'd forgotten about that, I might go as lad from 1913," Guy smiled, but his heart wasn't in it. The person he wanted to spend time with the most would not be at the party.

A car pulled up to the factory, bringing Guy and Angel back to the matter at hand. It was a large red car with the roof cover on, over spacious seats in the back. The headlamps and front grill were polished brass. The wheel spokes were red and a spare wheel was mounted by the drivers' door.

"Get ready Guy, I reckon this is it," said Angel pushing Guy in front of her. "It's quite bold, it will be easy enough to follow."

"Right, let's hope it doesn't go too fast and there is a lot of traffic to slow it down."

Without acknowledging the driver, Henry Towers got into the back of the car, it pulled away, slowly at first. Guy and Angel emerged from the alleyway, walking along pretending to ignore the car by pointing at the building opposite the factory. As the car turned the corner and gathered pace, Guy and Angel also sped up. Angel's boots made it difficult for her to run on the Manchester cobbles, but she did a good job of keeping up with Guy to begin with.

The car turned left and then right into Redhill Street and past the Tenney factory, Guy managed to keep up with car as it made its way along the canal and turned left into Swan Street. Here the road was busier, which worked in his favour, as the car had to keep stopping in among the horse drawn carts, bicycles and buses. The large red polished car did indeed stand out in the crowded Manchester roads.

Ducking into the shadows of the shops, Guy and Angel kept alongside the car and quickly darted across the road as the car suddenly turned off into Travis Street. Guy caught the car up as it was heading south into Baring Street, but here the road was much emptier, and the car picked up speed. Guy kept an eye on the car, although by now he had lost Angel.

Eventually the car pulled up outside a shop in between two small horse drawn carts, an old woman emerged from the car, wearing black from head to toe, she reminded Guy of Queen Victoria, except that she was wearing a large black hat with feathers drooping down at the sides. He caught up with the car and nonchalantly glanced inside, expecting to see Henry Towers in the back seat, but to Guy's surprise, he was not there. Guy did a double take and then turned to look this way and that around the street. Henry Towers was nowhere to be seen.

A huge puffing noise made Guy turn to see Angel arriving at the scene.

"I've lost him Angel, I could have sworn that I had an eye on his car all the way, but I must have lost it somewhere, probably at that left turn just now. Oh, for God sake, all that effort and he's slipped away home."

"It was a long shot, don't worry, we'll find another way," said Angel, bent over double trying to catch her breath. "Who else do we know that might be able to point us in the right direction of his house?"

"No one, just the Pankhursts, but there must be another way."

"Guy, I won't get involved with them and the whole blowing up the park thing, we could just..."

"Billy, John and Wilf, why didn't I think of them before?"

"Who?" said Angel, puzzled at Guy's

excitement.

"They boys I met outside the Towers' factory." Guy turned around to walk back the way they came.

"Oh, yes, would they know where he lives?" shrugged Angel following Guy.

"No harm in asking, let's go back, it's early evening, they might be playing out by now."

"Even if they're not there, someone who works in his factory must know where he lives," said Angel.

"I'm not running back."

"Good," replied Angel, still trying to catch her breath.

*

The little alleyway across from the factory was empty, but there were quite a few people in the street at the front of the houses.

"Who should we ask?" said Guy. "People might be a bit suspicious if we start asking where the Towers live, we don't want to be arrested."

Angel rolled her eyes and laughed. "No, we don't do we. Maybe I could strike up a conversation with one of the women and say how I would like to thank Letitia Towers."

"That might work, or we could go to a pub round here, that might help," said Guy, looking around for a pub. "Where would boys go to play this time of day?"

"Don't ask me, no idea," said Angel. "Although I can see the appeal of the canal towpath, it's quite exciting and bustling down there."

"Brilliant Angel, that's it, let's walk down by the canal."

They made their way to the towpath and had a look each way along the canal, they decided to walk left upon seeing a small group in the distance. The group, however, turned about to be some young barge workers with Irish accents, standing around chatting and smoking pipes as they waited for their barge to be given a signal to leave. Turning to walk in the opposite direction, Guy and Angel bumped into three boys running along excitedly chasing each other.

"Billy," called Guy.

Billy stopped and turned to look at Guy.

"Oh, it's you again, John, Wilf, look it's the man who gave us a penny," shouted Billy to his mates.

"Aye, hello, what you up to?" said Wilf.

"Well actually lads, you might be able to help me and my friend," Guy indicated to Angel.

The boys turned to stare at Angel.

"Is she your girlfriend?" asked Wilf.

"No just a friend," said Guy smiling at Wilf and turning to raise an eyebrow to Angel.

"How can we help?" said John.

"Well Mrs Towers was really kind to my friend, and we would like to take her some flowers, you know, to say thank you," said Guy, thinking quickly. "Do you know where the Towers live?"

"Ah no," said the boys together, looking at each other for inspiration and shaking their heads.

"No worries, thanks anyway," said Guy. "You boys have a nice evening, and don't do anything silly."

The boys laughed and turned to continue their chase, whilst Guy and Angel turned to begin walking back up to the street.

"Shall we try a pub then?" suggested Angel.

Before Guy could answer he felt a tug on his jacket and turned to see Billy.

"Me ma might know, she went there once to do some cleaning for Mrs Towers, she quite likes her," said Billy.

"Brilliant, Billy, where is your ma now?" said Guy. "Can I go and see her?"

"She'll be home from factory, I'll take you now if you like," said Billy, looking proud he was able to help.

"You are a star," said Angel. "Thank you so much."

*

"Mrs Taylor, it's lovely to meet you and thank you so much for your help," said Angel. "I really wanted to thank Mrs Towers personally for her help and now I can."

"It's really no problem, she is a true lady that one, never turns her nose up at us, not like 'er husband, dunno what she sees in 'im." Mrs Taylor smiled as she leant on her door frame. "Well, I must be getting on, but good luck."

Mrs Taylor went in and shut her door, leaving Guy and Angel in the street with Billy, John and Wilf.

"I think you deserve another penny each, for your help," said Guy.

The boys looked at each other and all shouted "chips" at the same time. Pennies in hand they ran off, presumably towards the nearest chippy.

"We can ask directions at the hotel," said Angel. "A huge yellow brick house should be easy enough to find though."

Guy and Angel began to wander back in the direction of the hotel, both quiet and pondering the confrontation with Henry Towers ahead of them. Angel linked her arm with Guy's and they walked on, through the gloom of the gas lit lamps and the fine drizzle that had dampened the cold night air.

"Are you thinking what I'm thinking?" said Guy.

"I don't know, if you are wondering what we do if he refuses to hand over the egg, then yes," replied Angel.

"Thought so," said Guy, squeezing Angel's arm, he then turned to face the road ahead, hoping the drizzle would mask his sad face.

*

About twenty minutes later, Guy and Angel paused, realising they had gone the wrong way. The road seemed to be much shabbier than other areas they had seen, and the smell of sewage mixed with the acrid smell of factory smoke was overwhelming.

"Do you know where we are?" asked Angel. "I don't recognise this at all."

"No, me neither, I think we need to retrace our steps a bit, this area is not improving the more I see of it." Guy looked in horror at the deprivation around him, it was the worst he had seen in 1913.

The redbrick houses were back-to-back, no alleyway in between them this time, giving a very closed in feel to the streets. He stared at the washing lines hung across the dirty, almost black walls from window to window, most of which were broken. The sheets and clothes seeming to be little more than dirty rags fluttering in what breeze there was and getting wet in the drizzle. Steps led down to unappealing cellar dwellings. Train viaducts bridged the roads, as trains rumbled by overhead, puffing and chugging adding to the sour smell in the air. Guy and Angel stepped to avoid what looked and smelled like raw sewage as rats ran by.

Children ran past them, barefooted, dirty and poorly clothed, running and chasing each other with little purpose to their game. Open mouthed they watched a man tumble out of a building and roll onto the cobbles in front of them, he seemed unaware of his plight, looking dazed as a woman shouted at him for being drunk. A group of men standing nearby, smoking pipes and huddled in conversation, turned to look at the commotion, looked at Guy and Angel and then turned away. The drunk man stood up and leered at Angel, saying something unintelligible. Guy pulled Angel close as they hurried on by getting further lost in the maze of gloomy and grim streets.

They came to a building that had a sign on it saying Charter Mission, Guy nodded in realisation of where they were.

"Angel Meadow," Guy said quietly.

"You know this place?"

"It's a commemorative park now, mum brought us here, I'm sure it's the same place. It's Angel Meadow."

"It sounds so lovely, like somewhere you would want to go to, but it looks and smells like hell."

They huddled together, stumbling on the wet cobbles, trying to find the route back to the main road and found themselves following some children along a dimly lit path, mesmerised by their squeals. They came to an open area with swings and watched as the children ran to the equipment, hanging on to the framework, waiting for a chance to have their turn.

"I'm sure this is the way back." Guy pointed to a gap in between the houses and led Angel away from the swings.

"Might as well try it," said Angel sadly, as they followed more children into the gap.

Irish Music was blaring out across the street from a pub. "The Exile of Erin," said Guy, "that's an unusual name for a pub."

Much laughter could be heard coming from inside the pub. "I can see now why people need to drink to dull the pain, this is not living, this is existing," said Angel, watching as two men began a street fight a little further on.

"Ok, up here, I think we are nearly out." Guy

led Angel up a slope, passing some women sitting on the steps outside of their house, shawls ripped and ragged, chatting away oblivious to the chaos of the street fight.

Finally finding their way out between two tall redbrick factories and realising where they had made their error, Guy and Angel paused to get their breath back and stop their hearts from beating so fast. As Manchester life carried on around them, they stood speechless, reflecting on the horror of the poverty they'd seen, tears sliding down their faces. They hugged for a moment, wiped their eyes and walked silently back to their hotel.

Chapter 16 – Wednesday 5th November 1913

"I can't see any yellow brick buildings, let alone a large house made of them," said Guy looking up and down Lower Park Road.

They had left the hotel at six thirty that morning, paying their bill and catching the bus in their finest clothes, all the way down to the Rusholme area of Manchester.

"Yellow brick and black window frames, with a large tree in the garden, that's what Mrs Taylor described," said Angel, craning her neck and switching her leather bag from one hand to the other. "Hang on, what's that? It's set back and slightly facing away from us, but I think that might be it."

They made their way towards the building Angel indicated could be the home of Mr and Mrs Towers. It was a gothic Victorian house, with huge bay windows on one side and a front door with a pointed porch rising above it. Either side of the front door, the walls rose to a pointed roofline, as they got closer, they could see that every door and window was framed with intricate brickwork and an elaborate chimney topped off the imposing building. The big red shiny car they had tried to follow the day before was parked on the drive and made an interesting colour clash with the yellow brick building.

"Well, if Henry Towers doesn't live here, I reckon the *Addams Family* do," said Guy taking in the house that stood out from the rest of the street.

"Who are they?" asked Angel, looking at the decoration above the doors and windows.

"They're a fictional TV family, *they're creepy and they're cooky, mysterious and spooky.*" Guy sang an old theme tune. "And I feel as nervous as if they did live here."

"They sound just like Henry; he is definitely a creep. Not Letitia though, I hope she isn't in on all this." Angel stopped walking as they reached the front door. "Oh well, here goes."

"*Once more unto the breach dear friends,*" said Guy, more nervously than he would have liked.

"I know that quote, it's Shakespeare, nice chap." Angel winked at Guy.

"What? Have you met…" but Guy was cut off as Angel rang the bell.

They both stood, awaiting their fate, for someone to come and answer the door, but no one did.

"Should we ring again?" asked Guy. "It feels rude though."

"It's rude to go stealing other people's property and smuggling ancient artefacts," said Angel, as she rang the bell again.

A minute later a maid opened the door, looking flustered in her black dress, with a white a pinafore and mop cap.

"Can I help you?" she said, her tone curt, she was clearly annoyed at the early morning callers.

Guy took his hat off. "We are so sorry to bother you, but we have urgent business with Mr Towers.

"He is currently breakfasting sir, I don't think he will see you now," replied the maid.

"We can wait until after he has finished breakfast," said Angel, smiling kindly at the maid.

The maid looked unsure what to do, she glanced nervously back into the house.

"Tell Mr Towers that we want to talk to him about Egypt," said Angel. "We can wait here for now," she added helpfully, trying to put the maid at ease.

The maid shut the door. Guy and Angel looked at each other with raised eyebrows. Would Henry Towers let them in? Would he take the bait?

"He might send some of his henchmen to see us off, crikey we didn't think of that," said Guy anxiously.

The door opened. "Mr Towers will see you in the library now," said the maid, opening the door wide and stepping aside to let them in.

"Let's hope it's not with the *rope or lead piping*," said Guy aside to Angel.

"That sounds awful, why would you say that?"

"It's from a game, ignore me." Guy laughed at his own joke, trying to distract himself from the confrontation to come.

It was not much warmer inside the house than outside, both Guy and Angel shivered as the maid led them across a wide black and white tiled entrance hall, with a sweeping staircase to the right and an elaborate chandelier in the middle. They made their way to a narrow hallway where the maid opened the door to a small room dominated by large windows. The bookshelves on the surrounding walls were full, mostly containing dusty old books. In the centre of the room was a large desk with a with a green leather top and a green lamp, with an angled head pointing over a large book that was open ready for reading. Inkwells and pens were also on the desk ready should anyone need to write a letter.

Henry Towers was stood leaning on a

winged red leather armchair by an unlit fireplace, face like thunder, he waved the maid away and looked Guy and Angel up and down,

"Who are you two? You madam, look familiar, explain yourselves," said Henry Towers with a scowl on his face that was rather intimidating.

"I am Miss Jasmine and this is my friend, Mr Devereux," said Angel, holding Henry Towers gaze with her own. "You met me last week at the suffragette reception in Manchester Town Hall."

"So I did, I might have known you were one of those hysterical women my wife wastes her time with." Henry Towers relaxed, now he could see his opposition, he clearly felt as though they posed no threat to him. "You want to talk to me about Egypt," he walked closer to them and stuck his neck out. "Go on then, what have you got to say."

"Well sir," began Guy. "You are importing ancient artefacts from Egypt illegally and selling them in London."

"You can't prove that!" said Henry Towers, almost laughing and dismissing the accusation.

"Actually, I have seen the blue stature with hieroglyphics on it and the black cat, that came in on Monday night," said Guy, taking a step forward towards Henry Towers, trying to show that he was not intimidated by him. "We know what you and

Tenney are up to, with your late-night shipments and we could go to the police now, even if they don't believe us, at the very least they will be watching you."

Running his hand through his hair, Henry Towers was taken aback and turned away from Guy and Angel.

"We are here to offer you a deal," said Angel.

"You mean blackmail me," said Henry Towers still facing the fireplace.

"Sort of, but we don't want money, we want the Faberge egg you stole from Beatrice Waibel in London," said Angel.

"It rightfully belongs to her and her family." Guy moved forward a little, feeling bolder as Henry Towers was rattled by their demands.

Henry Towers turned back to face the pair. "No, it does not belong to that woman, she tricked my aunt, the egg was promised to me since I was a small boy, she was a gold digger, plain and simple."

"I don't think she was a gold digger, Beatrice was very kind to your aunt, looking after her in her last few years." Angel moved forward to join Guy.

"Would she have been so kind if my aunt wasn't so rich? I doubt it." Henry Towers spoke through gritted teeth. "So, this is your little bribe is it, I give you the egg and you don't go to the police."

Guy and Angel did not reply, they just stood their

ground in front of Henry Towers, watching him mull the situation over in his mind. Angel reached into her bag and pulled out the statement they wanted him to sign.

"Is that an ownership statement? It will never stand up in a court of law." Henry Towers' demeanour had changed and he was now looking smug. "You two are nothing more than children, playing games in an adult world. I think you'll find that I will not be signing your letter of ownership, I will be keeping the egg and I will do what I please when it comes to Egyptian artefacts. So, you have had your fun, now be on your way, before I call some friends to help you on your way."

"Sir," said Angel. "Beatrice Waibel has a close relative, a child, that is very ill. The child needs an operation to save her, but the family have no money. That egg can be sold to pay for the operation and save the little girl's life."

"The family are desperate sir," pleaded Guy, beginning to feel as though the conversation was slipping away from them. "You have the power to save her life in your hands."

"Poppycock, a fairy story," said Henry Towers laughing and waving a dismissive hand towards them. "You could be making this up, a couple of con artists, confidence tricksters. I know your sort."

"Sir, we wouldn't come all the way from

London, track you down and stand before you if the Waibel family were not desperate," said Guy.

"Be on your way now, go, I have had enough of playing with children today." Henry Towers was becoming irritated again as he moved over to the window and looked out onto Lower Park Road.

After exchanging a glance with Guy, Angel pursed her lips and sighed, putting the statement back in the bag.

Henry Towers turned back and began walking to the desk, his cheeks red and his eyes bulging. "I said go, now." His voice was almost a hiss.

Worried that Henry Towers had a gun in the desk drawer, Guy pulled Angel towards him and they made their way to the door, they scuttled back across the hall, letting themselves out of the front door.

"Well, that didn't go well, did it?" said Guy breathless as they ran down the front path back to the road. "I suppose we could say that at least he knows we're on to him."

"I imagine his pals will be onto us soon too." Angel screwed her nose up and shuddered. "We're gonna have to be careful Guy, we must not get separated, not now."

"Agreed. The confrontation was never going to be easy, was it? He is a vile criminal at the end of the day."

"Stop, stop," called a voice, making them turn back to face the Towers' house, only to find the maid running up to them.

"Oh God, what now." Guy exchanged a worried glance with Angel as the maid reached them.

"Come back, Mrs Towers would like to talk to you."

*

The maid directed the pair back into the library, Guy and Angel found Letitia Towers standing by the desk, Henry Towers was seated in the armchair by the fireplace,

"My love," said Henry Towers, who was calmer now, "these children have just left, they have nothing of interest to say. Why have you called them back?"

"You two stay right there," ordered Letitia, staring at her husband. "I heard every word of that conversation from the bathroom above. You told me that was a one-off shipment, three months ago. You, Henry dear, cannot be trusted. My family are keeping your factory afloat, and you want to play at grave robbing from Egyptian tombs. You should be focused on cotton, Henry, cotton and the cotton industry. You're the child who never grew up, the spoilt child, who didn't want to work as hard as his parents did."

"Not at all Letitia, darling, do not listen to these money seeking children." Henry Towers was beginning to sound desperate.

"What I should have done is listened to my parents, you are every inch the scoundrel they said you were, but I was blinded by your charm," said Letitia, moving to stand over her husband. "And as for the Faberge egg, I thought that epic tale was over months ago. The courts found in Beatrice's favour, you lost, the egg belongs to her."

Letitia turned to face Guy and Angel. "Are you telling me, this awful husband of mine, stole the egg from Beatrice after all?"

"Not himself, he hired two men to steal the egg, they broke into her flat and her children had to hide under the bed, terrified for their lives," said Angel, getting Letitia Towers up to speed.

"Henry, darling," said Letitia sarcastically. "Be a good boy and fetch the egg now, you will then sign the letter of ownership immediately."

Henry Towers stared at his wife, lips shut tight together, but he didn't move.

"And when you have signed that, you will be signing another contract, I think you will find that my parents will move to get you off the board. From now on I will run the factory and you will be my employee; I will find you something suitable to do." Letitia Towers narrowed her eyes at her husband.

Still Henry Towers did not move from the armchair, his gaze remained on his wife as contemplated his future.

"You can have a job if you behave, otherwise you can go to prison and reflect on the price of a Faberge egg and study Egyptology from your cell." Letitia had all the cards, and she was playing them well. "Beatrice's family are in need, we have plenty, we do not need the Faberge egg, you are greedy, go and get it now before I call for Amy and she will call for the police. Your choice."

Henry Towers knew when he was beaten, he stood up and like a petulant child, stormed out of the room.

"Thank you Mrs Towers, once again I am indebted to you," said Angel. "I wanted to see you, to thank you for your evidence in court."

"You are very welcome. Mrs Pankhurst told me you were trying to track Henry down and that he had something belonging to a friend of yours. I had a feeling it would be the Faberge egg. He is like a magpie, collecting all things that glitter. I hope the egg helps the little girl to have her operation, it is going to a good cause."

Henry returned to the room with a small black velvet bag, which he put on the desk. Angel put the ownership statement on the desk too.

Letitia reached into the velvet bag and pulled out the original ownership document, laying it on the table beside the letter. She then returned to the bag and lifted out the egg itself, standing it on the desk.

"It's beautiful," gasped Angel, looking at the small but exquisite enamelled royal blue egg in front of her.

"It was made by Karl Faberge himself for Tsar Alexander III of Russia; it was originally intended as a gift for his oldest daughter Xenia's sixteenth birthday, which coincided with Easter. The Tsar used to give his wife a Faberge egg each Easter." As Letitia picked up the egg, the sun caught the gold, that ran down the curvature of the blue enamel. She then set the egg down on its little gold legs and traced her finger over the gold crown shaped finial at the top.

"Anyway, Henry's Uncle Charles was visiting at the time, he really did find the most beautiful silks to trade with. The Tsar was so pleased with silks he bought for his wife and daughters that he gave the egg to Charles by way of thanks."

"Aunt Elizabeth had no right to give it away," said Henry Towers defiantly.

"She had every right to give it away, it was hers and Beatrice was an angel sent from heaven in the last few years of Elizabeth's life. What did you ever do for Elizabeth? Except wait for her to pass, so that you could inherit. You inherited enough and wasted most of the money on your incompetent and greedy schemes. You are a fool Henry Towers and this beautiful egg belongs to Beatrice, now sign both of these documents before Amy calls for the police to take you away."

Picking up the pen and dipping it in the ink, clearly caused Henry Towers great pain. He signed the documents, his face red and his eyes almost tearful, he glared at his wife and his visitors and left the room without another word. Letitia returned the egg to the black velvet bag and after blotting the ink on the two documents, she folded them up and put them in the bag too. She pulled the drawstring tight and knotted it for extra safety.

"Please return this to Beatrice with my compliments and apologise for the behaviour of my husband. Her poor children must have been terrified, what an ordeal for them." Letitia Towers handed the bag to Angel. "I hope the operation comes in time and the little girl recovers well."

Angel put the velvet bag inside her own bag and snapped it shut as the trio left the library.

"Chloe is quite poorly," said Guy. "This will make a difference to her, I'm sure of it.

"Chloe, such a pretty name, from Greek mythology I believe," said Letitia Towers. "For

Chloe then. Will you head back to London now?"

"Straight away," said Guy as they made their way back across entrance hall to the front door.

Amy the maid opened the door for Guy and Angel, who gave their final farewells and thanks, before hurrying back down the path a second time to Lower Park Road.

*

The whistle blew, the steam clouded around the windows and the train chugged away from the wrought iron and glass ceiling of London Road station. Guy and Angel were sitting in a first-class compartment, they felt that it was safer to be alone, given their special luggage. The compartment had a sliding glass door out to a passageway and afforded them the privacy they needed. They flopped back in the seats facing each other and let out a huge sigh of relief as the train gathered pace.

"One of us will need to be awake at all times," said Guy, nodding towards Angel's bag.

"Definitely." Angel gripped the bag tight to her side.

"We've done it though, we've got the egg, I still can't believe it to be honest. Thank God for Letitia Towers, she is a star."

"I hope she gives Henry a rough time, he really should be in prison," said Angel looking out as Manchester was disappearing into the distance.

Guy joined Angel in watching the factories, chimneys and smoke fade into the distance. "Still can't believe I saw United play though."

Angel rolled her eyes and smiled, then reached into her bag getting out the magazines they had bought for the trip up to Manchester. "We can finish these now. I think our journey was just as epic as Scott in the Antarctic," she said referring to the front cover of *The Strand*. "Well, maybe not – it was warmer though, just!"

"Thanks," said Guy taking his magazine and settling in to read. "I'm not sure I was warmer when I was in the open carriage, heading to Stockport, with ancient Egyptian artefacts for company."

They both laughed, the horror of that night fast becoming a distant memory, as the train whistled and gathered even more pace.

*

It was late evening when the train pulled into Marylebone station, the lamplights twinkling beneath the steam as they ground to a halt. Guy and Angel made their way to the London Underground Station and looked at the map.

"Right, in my day we'd get the Circle or Metropolitan line back to Liverpool Street," said Guy tracing his finger along the map on the wall.

"It looks like we have to go one stop on the Bakerloo line and then pick up the Metropolitan line to Bishopsgate."

Looking at the signs they followed the tiled passages and soon found themselves on the platform. It wasn't long before a train arrived, they changed trains at Baker Street and were getting off at Bishopsgate before they knew it.

They emerged onto Bishopsgate Street, their breath visible in the cold air as they spoke, when a loud explosion made them jump, it was followed by what sounded like gunshots. Guy and Angel ducked into the nearest doorway and stood there frozen with fear, looking around in terror for the source of the explosions.

"Is it Towers?" Guy was breathless, angry and there was a hint of fear in his voice.

"Do you think his men are after us?" said Angel in alarm. "We knew it was a possibility."

As Angel turned to look at Guy, his expression changed to relief and he started to laugh, he laughed so much he was unable to explain why.

Angel was bemused. "I'm glad you find this funny, but please tell me why." She ducked every time she heard an explosion.

"Guy Fawkes," was all Guy could eventually say. "It's Guy Fawkes."

"Oh, I know about this, the Catholic plot to blow up the Houses of Parliament and the annual celebration of the plotters' brutal execution," said Angel relaxing. "To be honest I thought it was the Pankhursts and their park bombs at first."

They stood watching the fireworks as Guy regained his composure and Angel's pulse rate returned to normal.

"I don't know why I'm smiling, I am actually named after Guy Fawkes, well Guy the First was anyway, but fireworks are so entertaining aren't they. At school my friends used say I should be on the bonfire, every Bonfire Night, same old joke."

"Nice friends," said Angel pulling a face.

"They didn't mean it; I don't think so anyway. Shall we go, I still feel a bit on edge with that egg in your bag."

Back in Liverpool Street station they could see there was one last train out to Chalk Hill that evening and it was leaving in ten minutes.

"Talk about cutting in fine," said Guy as they ran to the platform, tickets in hand. "My last journey on a steam train, back to boring trains tomorrow."

They ran through the steam and jumped into yet another first-class carriage, a minute later the train pulled out into the night, heading towards the Chalk Hill and the twenty-first century.

As Guy and Angel were alone in their carriage, they chatted away about their adventure, from London Zoo, the cinema and Southend; to Manchester United and the Pankhursts.

"On behalf of Barbara and her family and especially Chloe, thank you for this, thank you for being arrested and thank you for being so brave and taking risks," said Guy leaning forward and holding Angel's gloved hands. "You are fearless."

"It's my pleasure and my job." Angel squeezed Guy's hands. "Anyway, you are quite fearless yourself, jumping on and off trains in the cold dark of the night.

"If you ever need a travelling companion, you know where I am." Guy let go of Angel's hands and sat back in his seat. "This isn't goodbye for good, is it?"

Angel smiled sadly and looked away. "To be honest I have no idea."

"So it could be." Guy choked on his words and looked at the floor. He was fighting the tears that were stinging at the back of his eyes.

They looked at each other, not knowing what to say, when a noise outside the carriage in the passageway made them look up. Two men were walking along and had bashed into the door of their compartment as the train jolted. The guard was hurrying the men along, but Guy and Angel recognised them instantly as the men that bumped into them at the Oval station.

"The thieves," they said in hushed voices, sighing in frustration.

"Henry Towers doesn't give up does he," said Guy angrily. "What is the matter with someone who puts their own greed over the need of a sick child?"

"He is awful, isn't he," agreed Angel, grabbing her bag close. "How far is it to Chalk Hill?"

"We just left Brentwood didn't we, the next station is Chalk Hill. About five minutes more I reckon."

"Guy, when we reach Chalk Hill, run, just run in any direction that you know will be safe for me drop you back."

"Ok, yes, ok I can do that. What about the egg?"

"Don't worry about that, I will see to it."

The train whistled and steam blew along outside the windows, as it began to slow on its approach to Chalk Hill station. Guy and Angel stood up, smiling nervously at each other.

"Ready?" said Angel.

"Ready." Guy nodded, his heart racing as he

opened the sliding door to the passageway and looked nervously around to see if the men were there. They weren't.

They walked along the passage to the door that would open onto the platform, looking around them the whole time. Even before the train had quite stopped Guy had opened the door.

"Bye Angel," he said fighting the tears, and then he was gone, disappearing into the steam and charging down the platform to the exit.

Guy ran through the ticket barrier, chancing a look behind him. Angel was in pursuit and behind her the two men were getting off the train.

"Don't stop Guy," yelled Angel. "Keep running."

Guy obeyed, running out of the station across the road and heading to the village green in the centre of Chalk Hill. As he reached the green, he felt himself being lifted up in the air. Once more he spun around in the eye of the little cyclone before gently heading back down to the ground.

Chapter 17 – Sunday 23rd October

The brown leather bag was beside Guy on Chalk Hill village green, where he was sitting trying to get his breath back. He looked in the bag and found his running gear, Garmin watch and his phone. Guy looked at the time, it was about three minutes after he had left two weeks ago. Inside Angel's bag he could see the black velvet pouch was there. There were also some paper leaflets, he pulled them out to find Angel's *Sketch*, his Manchester United programme and *The Strand* magazine. Guy laughed and cried at the same time.

"Thank you, Angel, I'm gonna miss you more than you will ever know."

Wiping the tears from his eyes, Guy got to his feet and went over to the public toilet. He changed into his running clothes, washed his face, packed his 1913 clothes into Angel's bag and began to make his way back home to the Lakeview Estate.

*

"Is that you Guy?" called Grandma as he shut the front door. "Hurry up and have shower, I'm just dishing up."

Guy laughed, the roast dinner he had thought so much about, was just being served. "Will do," he replied.

"You absolutely pong," said Mark, walking past, not looking up, face glued to a game on his phone and earphones in, barely visible under his mop of curly brown hair.

"I imagine I do; they don't have deodorant in 1913," replied Guy to the oblivious Mark.

Guy walked into his bedroom and shut the door, he dropped Angel's bag on his bed, then thought better of it and hid the bag at the back of his wardrobe. He went to the bathroom and took a quick shower, enjoying the hot running water and shower gel, used some deodorant, got dressed and went downstairs to join his family for a roast dinner. It was surreal, like the last two weeks hadn't happened, no time had passed on this adventure. He was back where he had started, but he was in possession of the long lost Faberge egg.

*

After dinner Guy shut his bedroom door and took Angel's bag from his wardrobe. He took out his 1913 clothes.

"Dry cleaners for you lot and you'll do for

the fancy dress party," he said to himself, putting them in a sports bag.

He took out the two magazines and the signed football programme and put them in an old shoebox containing, football programmes from his childhood. He put the shoebox back on a on high shelf and turned his attention back to the bag. The only thing left in the bag was the black velvet pouch with the egg inside. Guy took the egg out of the pouch and looked at in detail. It really was a beautiful jewel, thought Guy as he turned it around under the light.

"I need to get you to Barbara tomorrow, but how am I going to do that without her knowing who is giving it to her," Guy sighed. "Let's give this some thought. There must be a way."

Guy got undressed, threw his pyjama shorts on and jumped into bed, glad to be able to sleep somewhere familiar and even more glad to have his own pillow. He turned out the light and thought about his conundrum for about half an hour, satisfied he had the answer, he set his alarm and allowed sleep to drift over him.

Chapter 18 - Monday 24th October

The alarm went off at four, Guy sat up and took a deep breath. "Right, here goes."

Rummaging around in his draw, he found some clean running kit and a hoodie. He grabbed Angel's bag, crept out of his bedroom, down the stairs and out of the front door, very glad it was still dark. Guy walked quickly into the village and along the little lane where Barbara's cottage sat in a row of three others.

"I hope she doesn't have a *Ring* doorbell," he said to a fox that crossed his path.

He caught his reflection in a window and realised he looked like a burglar with the bag in his hand. Guy went up to the front door and looked around to check no one was about.

"I'm sorry about this Barbara, but it is for

the greater good," he whispered to himself as he used the doorbell, which thankfully was the old-fashioned type without a camera.

He rang the bell several times then ran across the road hiding in the hedge opposite. Guy wanted to check Barbara heard the bell ring, he felt dreadful waking her up so early in the morning, but it was the only way to return the egg anonymously.

After a minute Guy saw a light go on in the upstairs bedroom, then the curtain twitched. Another minute or so and Barbara opened the front door in her dressing gown, her husband Frank at her side, they looked around nervously. Then Barbara spotted the bag at the door, she went to grab it, but Frank pulled her back. Guy could see them having a discussion. Frank bent down and opened the bag, he felt inside and pulled out the black velvet bag. Frank and Barbara looked at each other puzzled.

Frank unknotted the drawstring and Barbara reached inside pulling out the pieces of paper. She tried to read them, but didn't have her correct glasses, she handed the paper to Frank. He read them aloud and Barbara covered her mouth with her hand, her other hand clutching Frank's arm, she then felt inside the bag and pulled out the Faberge egg, shaking her head. Guy heard Barbara scream for joy as they shut the front door.

"Angel, I hope you saw that," said Guy looking up to the moon. "Wherever you are, thank you, you just made a family's dream come true."

Epilogue

"What you up to?" said Mark, barging into Guy's bedroom, earphones hanging round his neck and phone in hand.

"Hey, squirt, knock before you come in," said Guy shutting his laptop lid and glaring at Mark.

Mark ignored Guy's irritation. "Mum has just heard that Chloe is on the way to the airport with her mum and dad. Barbara said the doctors are really hopeful that the operation will be a success."

"The crowd funding worked well didn't it, all that money raised so quickly, overnight almost." Guy chuckled before he went on. "I hear Barbara is planning to give the money raised by the sale of the egg to Great Ormond Street Hospital, what a lovely thing to do!"

Mark sat on Guy's bed. "Bit of a weird one that, a mystery stranger knocking on Barbara's door in the middle of the night and leaving a bag with a very rare and expensive jewelled egg in it. One that has been missing for over a hundred years."

"It certainly is weird," agreed Guy, "but great though."

"And who is our resident, mysterious treasure hunter? Oh you."

"I'm not sure when I had the time to do that," laughed Guy.

"Neither am I," said Mark. "However, you were seen on that Sunday evening coming out of the public toilets on the village green with a leather bag."

"What? When I was out for a run," laughed Guy. "Well, it wasn't me, I haven't got a leather bag, and if I did have one, why would I take it out for a run?"

Mark looked at Guy and turned his head to the side. "Well, I don't know how you did it, but I know you did." Mark pointed two fingers at his own eyes and then one finger at Guy, to indicate he was watching him.

"You're ridiculous," said Guy as Mark left his bedroom laughing and nodding his head.

With Mark gone, Guy opened his laptop and resumed his research into the suffragettes in 1913, he had been wondering if the park bombings ever took place. What he found out was that there had been a large pipe bomb explosion in Manchester at Alexandra Park on 11th November 1913. Four days later on the 15th November, there was a bomb attack at Sefton Park in Liverpool at the Palm House.

"Wow, narrow miss there Angel," said Guy to his laptop. "They were certainly very determined women."

"I wonder, what happened to Henry Towers?" Guy typed his name and Manchester into a search engine. Looking at the results, he chose the option that led him to the *Commonwealth War Graves Commission* website, the name Henry Horatio Joseph Towers was linked to Lower Park Road, Manchester. "Definitely him them," mused Guy.

He clicked on the name and found out that Henry Towers had been killed during the Battle of the Somme in July 1916. Guy was shocked, he had not been expecting that news, he sat back in his chair and shook his head. Henry Towers was not a pleasant man, but he died fighting for his country.

"People are complicated Angel," said Guy looking up. "Oh, that's it, that's why no one found the egg. Henry Towers hadn't told anyone where the egg was, and it had just stayed hidden because he didn't return from the war. We thought that might be the case." Guy paused. "Wow, I know he was the villain in this story, but I wouldn't wish him to die in the trenches."

Guy then took a deep breath, he was on the website now, he knew had to check, the three boys from Manchester had been on his mind. He typed in Billy Taylor, then deleted Billy and typed in William. Nothing that emerged that seemed to fit the profile of a Billy or William Taylor in Manchester, this hopefully indicated that Billy did not die in the war.

"Well that's a relief and I don't know the other boys' surnames."

Guy relaxed, then he remembered Stephen Dracott, the young man he met at the Hotel Victoria, who wanted to be a chef in the future. Again, nothing returned on the war graves website, suggesting that Stephen was not killed in World War One.

"Good, good, I wonder what you did from 1914 to 1918," said Guy breathing another sigh of relief.

Guy then turned to a search engine and typed in Letitia Towers, there was a *Wiki* page about her. Guy found out how when the war started, she went out to France as nurse and worked at various dressing stations for four years. After the war she was a widow because Henry had died, but she did not hide away. She sold the cotton factory and set up a charity for underprivileged children in Manchester. During World War Two, she turned her house into a rehabilitation hospital for soldiers recovering from their injuries. She had died in 1965, with a local reputation in Manchester for being a philanthropist.

"What a woman she was Angel," said Guy, hoping Angel could hear. "Suffragette, cotton mill owner, World War One nurse and by the looks of it a World War Two nurse as well. She looked after others her entire life and fought for those in need, amazing."

Guy returned to the search engine page and typed in Sarah Clarke, Suffragette. A story emerged from a Mancunian newspaper about Sarah in November 1913 being arrested for her part in vandalism of a church, Ceclia Turner and Mary Crowley were mentioned in the article too, but there was no mention of Angel Jasmine. Guy wandered if Angel had worked her magic and deleted the story, or whether they just didn't report her as she was not found guilty.

"I guess I'll never know, will I?" said Guy laughing and shaking his head as he remembered the court room. "Angel, you have certainly put me through it the last few months."

Guy knew he needed to stop talking to Angel, but he missed her and it helped, he hoped the need would fade overtime.

Nothing else came to light on the Internet about Sarah, so returning to the search engine, Guy wondered how to look for Ottomar Waibel, even though he knew that Ottomar died fighting in the war. A few clicks here and there, but each option just came to a dead end.

"I wonder what your story was Ottomar," said Guy looking at the screen unable to translate the German on the webpage. "You, Billy, Henry, Stephen, Letitia and Sarah, I bet you all have interesting stories to tell about World War One, but I really don't fancy Angel taking me back to find out. So that research will have to wait for another time."

With that, Guy shut his laptop, changed into his running gear and was soon running down to the reservoir to clear his head and practice skimming stones.

Historical Context

Inspiration for Guy, Angel and the Missing Egg came whilst I was researching my own family tree. Ottomar and Beatrice Waibel are based on my own great-grandparents. They lived in London in 1913, in Coronation Buildings and Ottomar was indeed a German waiter at a Gordon's Hotel. Ottomar, sadly, did die at the Battle of the Somme in 1916. He had been deported back to Germany and his only way of seeing his English family again was to survive the First World War, he didn't.

In the 1900s there were many German waiters living and working in London, their reputation for waiting was second to none.

In this book, Guy and Angel found themselves involved with the suffragettes and the Pankhurst family. The suffragette activity described in the book is real, the conversations with the Pankhursts are not. We also hear in the book about the wider suffragist movement and the work of Millicent Fawcett, whose statue resides in

Parliament Square, Westminster, London.

Guy and Angel Travel in Time

Out now

Book 1 - Guy, Angel and the Devereux Legacy
Book 2 - Guy, Angel and the Missing Egg
Book 3 - Guy, Angel and the Emerald Necklace

Coming soon

Book 4 - Guy, Angel and the Elusive Painting
Book 5 - Guy, Angel and the Essex Outlaw
Book 6 - Guy, Angel and the Final Quest

About the Author

Often found running around London and the home counties, Dr. Chris Crawley is a historian and teacher, who loves to travel and dreams of being transported (for a short while) to the past.

Dr. Chris Crawley has a BA in History, and both a MA and an EdD in Education. She has been writing as a hobby for many years.

The Guy and Angel Travel in Time Series is her first set of books.

Let the journey continue...

Printed in Great Britain
by Amazon